CLASSIC MODERN HOMES OF THE THIRTIES

CLASSIC MODERN HOMES OF THE THIRTIES

64 Designs by Neutra, Gropius, Breuer, Stone and Others

JAMES FORD and KATHERINE MORROW FORD

DOVER PUBLICATIONS, INC., New York

Published in Canada by General Publishing Company, Ltd., 30 Lesmill Road, Don Mills, Toronto, Ontario.
Published in the United Kingdom by Constable and Company, Ltd.

This Dover edition, first published in 1989, is an unabridged and unaltered republication of the work originally published by Architectural Book Publishing Co., Inc., New York, in 1940 under the title *The Modern House in America.*

Manufactured in the United States of America
Dover Publications, Inc., 31 East 2nd Street, Mineola, N.Y. 11501

Library of Congress Cataloging-in-Publication Data

Ford, James, 1884–1944.
    [Modern house in America]
    Classic modern homes of the thirties : 64 designs by Neutra,
      Gropius, Breuer, Stone, and others / James Ford and Katherine
      Morrow Ford.
        p.   cm.
    Reprint. Originally published: The modern house in America. New
      York, N.Y. : Architectural Book Pub., c 1940.
    Includes index.
    ISBN 0-486-25927-7
    1. Architecture, Domestic—United States—Designs and plans.
      2. Architecture, Modern—20th century—United States—
      Designs and plans.   3. International style (Architecture)—
      United States. I. Ford, Katherine Morrow, 1905– . II. Title.
NA7208.F6   1989
    728.3'7'0973—dc 19   88-38596
                                                        CIP

CONTENTS

PREFACE

THERE is abundant evidence of a rapidly developing interest in the new architecture—known as modern. Recent polls by magazines (e.g. "Life" and the "Architectural Forum") make this clear. Also it is certain that increasing space would not long have been given to homes of modern design in the daily press, architectural and building journals, women's magazines, and periodicals in the field of home decoration in the absence of a sustained and developing popular demand.

This does not represent a trivial change in public taste, nor is it essentially a fad. The trend is not superficial but fundamental, not local but general. Its development is the natural result of the profound social and economic changes which have been running their progressive course within the past century. Above all it is a logical outgrowth of a new perspective upon human interests and values.

The purpose of this volume is threefold: to call attention to a movement which we believe to be of deep significance both to architecture and to life; to show it in its international perspective but with reference to America's contribution; and to make some of its potentialities known to home builders as well as to architects. Modern residential architecture has been treated as organic planning integrated with suitable design. This collection is essentially American, not merely because limited to houses built in this country, but because virtually every house presented shows some degree of American originality.

In the illustrated pages which follow, selection has been made of houses which exemplify the purposes and spirit, as well as the techniques, of modern architecture. Houses in which the forms, characteristic of modern, have served merely as a veneer or style, to hide a traditional plan, have been excluded as "modernistic," as distinguished from true or organic modern. Limitations of space, however, forced from the very outset the elimination of many excellent examples of new architectural design and of functional planning—houses that we would have liked to include. It was decided to omit all of the work of Frank Lloyd Wright, because illustrated accounts of the latter are available to the public in other volumes. On the other hand catholicity of representation seemed desirable in order that the regionalism of modern might be apparent, as well as the wide variety of interpretations, materials, and costs. A few of the earlier examples of the so-called "international style" were retained to reveal trends and transitional stages. We believe study of this collection by dates or sequence as well as by regions and by architects, to be profitable.

Examination of each house plan, in conjunction with the brief statement which accompanies it, should make it clear how each house grows out of the life and interests of its owner or tenants. This is particularly true of the houses designed in the later nineteen thirties. No house can be judged fairly without prior examination of the data concerning family composition and requirements, site, materials, and special features.

The authors, realizing that much good work in modern residential design in America has not yet been brought to public attention, hope that such examples will be called to their notice.

We wish to thank all architects who submitted material, whether or not it proved possible to include it in these pages, and all with whom we have had the privilege of correspondence or discussion. We are especially grateful to Howard Myers, Editor of the "Architectural Forum," for encouragement and constant interest and for many courtesies extended to us throughout the period in which our data and illustrations were being assembled. We are indebted to the "Architectural Forum," "Architectural Record," and "The Museum of Modern Art" for their generosity in lending material for reproduction; to Condé Nast Publications, Inc., for reproduction rights as indicated; and to all photographers and publishers for their kind cooperation.

To Professor Walter Gropius, Chairman of the Department of Architecture of the Graduate School of Design of Harvard University, and to Dr. Sigfried Giedion, General Secretary of the International Congress of Modern Architecture, we wish to express deep appreciation for frequent aid and guidance in making our selections of much of the material in these pages. We assume, however, full responsibility for the final selection.

James Ford

Katherine Morrow Ford

Lincoln, Massachusetts
April, 1940

WHAT IS MODERN?

THE essence of the new residential architecture is revealed in its twofold purpose: to base its plans upon the organic life of the family to be housed, and to make logical use of the products of invention. It has elected to make a fresh approach, to free itself of constraints, by consciously ignoring tradition and the expectations which the latter imposes with regard to facade and plan. The outer form of the modern house becomes the outgrowth of a plan built about the interests, routine activities, and aspirations of the client and his family expressed in terms of materials employed. Thus human need comes first. In skilful hands new appropriate and beautiful forms may emerge from an architecture which, discarding styles, lets the house grow from the inside outwardly to express the life within.

PERIODS IN ARCHITECTURE

Architecture like other arts has had several brief periods characterized by creative genius which established new forms. Such was the Periclean age in Greece from which the classic forms of our monumental architecture still largely derive. Such was also the Gothic period, still greatly influencing the design of our places of worship. Other great moments of Egyptian, Byzantine or other origin, as well as the continental Renaissance produced radical changes in design and construction. In the days of the great masters enduring works of beauty were left behind to inspire succeeding generations.

THEIR SOCIOLOGICAL BASIS

Outstanding genius is rare in every art, and appears to be a phenomenon of periods of radical social change wherein the opportunities for original self-expression are facilitated by the milieu. Discontent with things as they are and a new vision of the world as it might be are combined with the gift for analysis and fresh synthesis and the will to achieve. The absence of any one of these factors may make the change abortive. Their presence, when economic and social conditions are appropriate, may, under a leadership practical but inspired, produce a new era.

CONTEMPORARY REVOLT IN THE ARTS

In each of the great arts today there is abundant evidence of revolt. Old and stereotyped forms are being discarded. Experimentation in new modes of expression is taking varied forms. The future is not clear to the contemporary, but evidence that this is an age of transition is incontrovertible. One may sense sorrow and anguish but also courage and faith in the music of a Tchaikovsky, Sibelius, Stravinski, or Ravel. New forms are reflective of existing conditions and prophetic of the better conditions which are in process of germination. For the present is a period of social upheaval, continuously disturbing and at times terrifying. It invades the daily life of all sensitive persons with inescapable cogency. All of the arts, like music, respond to its impact. Much of contemporary poetry, literature, painting and sculpture appears to be overwhelmed by the tragedy of our times. Even in negation and rebellion one can detect the emergence of new prophetic art forms.

The industrial arts and living architecture in recent years display a freedom happily little contaminated by bitterness or by morbid fantasy. Theirs may be the vanguard of the aesthetic reformation. For they find the elements of the new order at hand and their vision is clear.

The new architecture like the other arts began also in revolt. It seeks to break the self-imposed restraints of the traditional forms. For in architecture as in other arts, the cycles which culminate in the birth of genius have always trailed off in slavish and uninspired reproduction of the designs of the greater masters. Thus at the turn of the century civic architecture in America was governed by Greek, Romanesque, Renaissance or Colonial traditions. Domestic architecture produced chiefly neo-classic or bastard Colonial, French, Spanish, Dutch or English styles. Industrial architecture alone displayed much freedom, for which necessity and engineering skills were largely responsible. Elsewhere traditional facades determined the plan behind them. Traditional materials and processes precluded needed innovations. Wide departure from accepted styles was not merely termed "bad taste"; it was feared and deplored.

REVOLT FROM TRADITIONAL ARCHITECTURE

All new movements have their germinal source in the past. One can trace the tap root of modern architecture to the industrial revolution which in America began its process of profound economic and social change more than a century ago. The use of steam power in industry not only made possible huge population aggregates and vast national wealth, but it also stimulated rapid invention in machine production and assembly of articles and products previously made by hand.

ECONOMIC GENESIS

Synthetic materials, prefabrication of the parts of the house, new processes, and vastly enlarged markets were but a few of the logical consequences of power-driven machinery. To the industrial revolution and its developments in engineering, in public utilities, and in merchandising, may also be traced the vast changes in the fundamental equipment of the home. The modern kitchen and bathroom, and modern heating, lighting, plumbing, refrigeration, water supply and sanitation are the synthetic products of thousands of individual inventions. To these may be added the more tardily arriving insulation against heat and cold, air conditioning, soundproofing, termite and vermin proofing, fireproofing, and waste disposal systems to safeguard man's health and comfort.

EFFECTS OF INVENTION

Meanwhile the mode of family life has changed. Within the century the home which had once been the seat of abundant arts and crafts lost these functions one by one. First sloughing off weaving, shoe and candlemaking the urban family more recently has given up laundering, preserving, and much of dressmaking and cooking for the purchase of mass-produced goods and services. Man's space needs within the home

CHANGE IN MODES OF LIVING

have thus been reduced to a fraction of their former proportions, with the resultant elimination of attics, sheds, storage cellars, work rooms, sewing rooms and laundry. Public provision of libraries, schooling, music, and recreation cause still further reduction of space needs for many homes. Easy access to shops reduces the size of storage space—closets, pantries—and kitchens. Outside entertainments and the restlessness induced by the pressures of an industrial civilization reduce the space needs for domestic social life. The family has declined also in size. There are fewer children, and it is becoming less common for three generations to live under one roof. Of late, standard prefabricated equipment and labor-saving devices so greatly reduce the old-time toil and inconveniences of housework that greater leisure is available to women, children are relieved of excessive household chores, and both can share in the new leisure which law and custom are affording to man.

MODERN ARCHITECTURE ACCEPTS THE CHALLENGE

Modern residential architecture thus makes its drastic innovations by means of recognition of two facts: that (1) radical changes in modes of living necessitate equally thoroughgoing changes in house planning; and that (2) the ever-increasing products of invention, in a highly industrial age, necessitate radical reformulation of modes of construction. These issues which have received some incidental attention in recent homes of traditional type, become primary in the new architecture.

Instead of a standard plan behind a standard, symmetrical front, the new architecture offers a nonstandard plan, commonly asymmetrical, developed after close study of the family's habits and interests. The exterior design is a logical outgrowth of the plan. The prevalent phrase "form follows function" thus connotes the abandonment of "style" for the logical three dimensional expression of family individuality.

INTERNATIONAL "STYLE" A MISNOMER

The term "international style" is consequently a misnomer when applied to the work of the leaders in the new architecture. For the forms which it takes are not a "style" except in the uninspired work of amateurs who, unaware of the spirit or meaning of modern architecture, copy what they will of its superficial manifestations. It would be calamitous to imprison the growth and freedom of the new architecture of the masters within the word "style" which puts a boundary around it. The spirit of living architecture is however essentially international.

HONEST USE OF MATERIALS

Although the designers of "period" houses may use the products of recent invention —equipment, prefabricated parts, and new materials—these tend to be mere accessories, leaving the standardized form virtually unchanged. To insurgent architecture, however, each of these offers opportunity for new expression. The mode of use may translate the characteristics of the material in question. Materials and fixtures derived from modern technology lose value when encased in traditional forms. Modernists consider it absurd that concrete should be made to look like natural stone, or electric light fixtures like candlesticks. Each in its use may honestly reveal its peculiar nature and purpose. The new materials make possible thinner walls, lighter construction, new proportions, and new textures. Again, and in quite another sense, it is seen that "form follows function." For the functions of materials as well as of human beings are susceptible of penetrating analysis, and of interpretation by means of architectural design. True beauty is never a veneer but always implicit in the material and its appropriate use.

The new architecture has been dubbed utilitarian by some of its opponents. If the term intends to damn the movement as materialistic it is singularly inept since no movement in design displays more of fervent though rationalized idealism. But if the term is used to connote the primacy of serviceability, and if the service to be rendered is to the whole man, then the new architecture is essentially utilitarian. For it caters not only to man's convenience and efficiency but also to his self-respect and his need for varied sociality, to his pursuit of cultural interests and of beauty. The coming generation may shake off its complacent acceptance of pseudo-classic fronts when it recognizes utilitarian forms in this broader sense.

SERVICE-
ABILITY

Modern architecture then seeks not style but substance, not ornament or ostentation but rational simplicity, not standard plans and facade but proficiency in exposition, not fitting the family to the house but the house to the family, not imitation but creation. Ideally it strives to make its fresh approach to the problem of design by the study of the latest findings concerning the nature of man and of social trends. It seeks fresh achievement in construction by thorough understanding and mastery of new materials and processes and of their potentials in use. It studies intensively the client and the members of the household, the site and its neighborhood, the available local organizations and materials for construction, and attempts an individualized synthesis which will perfect the adaptation of the dwelling to man. The resultant house is not a "machine for living," but a perceiving utilization of machine products to ease, facilitate, and even inspire each process of daily living for each member of the family.

STANDARDS
OF THE NEW
ARCHITECTURE

It is characteristic of all good residential architecture that it should provide for man's seven fundamental housing needs: health, safety, convenience, comfort, privacy, beauty, each with due reference to economy. Modern architecture has, however, made a fresh analysis of these needs and has not been forced into the compromises so frequently dictated by other architectural forms. Since it is free to develop its plans from a close study of the interests of each member of the household instead of first considering what architectural style to apply, the plan may become the logical solution of the family's needs. Just as the flower or tree is the logical development of the potentials of the seed, so the modern house seeks to be the organic expression of the interests and potentials of the family for which it is built. It develops outwardly from the core or center of family living.

FAMILY ANALYSIS Specifically needs may run the gamut of work and play, domestic life and social life, chores and hobbies, love and worship, meditation and inspiration—not forgetting the obvious routines and rituals of sleeping, bathing, dressing, eating, and catching the commuters' train. Hence the consideration of the areas of family life under such groupings as service areas, sleeping areas, living areas, and recreation areas. Each of these may require many subdivisions but is planned as an operative unit for its specific purpose, carefully interrelated with each other area within the house. This is a wide departure from earlier types of planning in which each room tended to serve as a cellular unit with under-emphasis upon correlation, circulation, and "flow of space." Though there is obvious need of efficiency in all household operations, there remains the more deeply seated requirement that the home should as far as possible facilitate creative living on the part of each individual while coordinating the lives within the household in reasonably progressive unity. Architecture is truly organic only in so far as it can protect personal privacy for the pursuit of any interest, from invasion, while preserving the organic whole.

LOCATION ANALYSIS Peculiarly characteristic of modern architecture is the measured adaptation of both the house and lot to the man—the attention paid to orientation for the warming rays of winter sunshine and protection from the more intense rays of the summer; to the placement of windows, doors, decks, and terraces, to take advantage of the vistas which nature offers, while protecting the family from the curiosity or intrusion of neighbors or passersby. In warm and temperate climates there has also been a high development of the "indoor-outdoor house" through which the indoor space is enlarged by its unobstructed view of the out-of-doors afforded by means of large glazed areas, which can at will be thrown open. The sense of confinement is correspondingly eliminated. For those who are sensitive to Nature's moods the way is continuously open to aesthetic appreciation and to spiritual stimulation.

Intrinsically, the modern house seeks to fulfil the implicit goal of housing, which is not mere shelter but the opportunity for unhampered and gracious living.

GEOGRAPHICAL DISTRIBUTION More than half the states have examples of good modern dwellings. California easily leads in number. The Atlantic seaboard states considered together nearly equal the output of the Pacific states. There is much modern residential design in the Great Lakes region, especially Michigan, Illinois and Ohio, and an appreciable increase of modern in the past three or four years in the southernmost area, notably in Florida, Texas, and Arizona. The remaining examples are widely scattered.

That new forms in architecture should originate in and spread from the periphery of our nation rather than its interior is probably accounted for chiefly by the fact that our greatest cities were established, for reasons of trade, where there were good natural harbors. The architects of modern carry on their profession in or near great metropolitan centers—Boston, Chicago, Los Angeles, New York, Philadelphia, San Francisco—where the cultural stimulation of urban life facilitates creative enterprise and where clients more readily experiment with new forms.

There may be additional explanations, however, in three other characteristics common to these areas. The first is the presence of outstanding natural beauty of sea, lakes, rivers or mountains which encourage the fenestration peculiar to modern design and yet may readily ensure privacy by means of screening vegetation. The second is the cultivation of outdoor living and the constructive use of leisure stimulated by both the wealth and the opportunities afforded by these regions. The third is a cultural derivation of multiple origin; the growing eagerness for simplicity, naturalness and wholesomeness of daily living, without sacrifice of the conveniences made available by modern technology, to which the urbanized client has become accustomed. For the clients themselves are chiefly persons of an urban or cosmopolitan culture who seek to recondition and promote their productiveness by a freer mode of living and by the inspiration which close, continuous contact with nature affords.

It is, however, a reasonable sociological presumption that from these urban coastal centers of radiation and their adjacent schools (e.g. Taliesin, Harvard, Columbia, University of California), the new architecture will spread to the rest of America. Indeed, it has already begun to do so. Viewed in terms of leadership, the architects fall with very few exceptions into two groups: the teachers and their followers. Excluding for the moment Frank Lloyd Wright, founder and Nestor of the new residential architecture, two clearcut groupings are observable, the men over forty years of age who are largely of European birth or training, and the men in their late twenties or early thirties who studied under the first group in office or school. Wright, carrying into residential design the teachings of Sullivan, is the acknowledged originator of the revolt from the traditional, of the spirit of new design, and of many of the radical new forms of construction. His disciples at Taliesin have been numerous and his influence continuous. Nevertheless that influence, which was more marked in Europe than America in the first three decades of this century, returned to this country under a new group of teachers and practitioners, modified by experiments and de-

LEADERSHIP

veloping experience under Gropius and Mies van der Rohe in Germany, Le Corbusier in France, Oud in Holland, and others.

Much interpenetrating influence of related arts and applied sciences, particularly of cubism and abstract art, of craftsmanship, industrial design and interior decoration, of city planning, housing and household economy, of invention in building products and processes, can be noted in this formative period. Art, science and life were consciously integrated in the education of the architect at the Bauhaus in Dessau, Germany.

Then came the hegira to America. In their relative youth came Belluschi, Lescaze, Neutra, Schindler, and Soriano, each prior to 1930. In more recent years arrived such already established leaders as Gropius—the founder of that pioneering school, the Bauhaus—and his associates, Breuer and Moholy-Nagy; also Mies van der Rohe from Germany, Saarinen from Finland, and Ruhtenberg from Sweden.

These men have been quick to catch the spirit of America, to appraise its opportunities for new rationales and mediums, and for new uses of materials. They are now making their own performance essentially American. They and their students are producing, not an "international style," but a new American architecture, cosmopolitan in spirit, but native both in form and detail—a genuine expression of American individuality.

Within this movement there has been originality in interpretation, and continuous progress from year to year. Thus the houses of 1938 and 1939 reveal a considerable departure from and frequent improvement upon those built prior to 1934. They show also more of Americanism as distinguished from the plagiarism from European models apparent in a number of houses designed more than five years ago.

America, which in the person of Wright took the leadership in modern architecture, thus yielded first place to Europe for the first three decades of this century. It is only within the past few years that leadership has been resumed in this country. Due to the constriction imposed in Europe upon all peaceful arts, by the conditions of a second world war, the future of the movement may rest with the younger generation of architects in the Western Hemisphere. In the United States they have so far demonstrated considerable capacity to escape equally the perils of reversion to traditionalism and the cliches of "moderne" or other unwarranted stylism, and also to avoid stereotyping unduly their own personal vocabularies in design. There appears to be evidence in the following pages of the existence of competence to accept this world challenge. They may make America for many years to come both source and custodian of all major developments in the new architecture.

ILLUSTRATED

PRESENTATION

OF

HOUSES

All Photos: Lynton Vinette

HOUSE FOR MR. AND MRS. C. H. EDWARDS, LOS ANGELES, 1936

Family Composition. Young couple. Fond of outdoor living.

Site. Level lot. Filled ground. Particular problem was the street, which loops around 3 sides of the lot. Privacy dependent on planting.

Construction. 8" x 8" posts, 8' on centers in living room, anchored to foundation by steel straps to act as vertical cantilevers for resistance against earthquake stresses. This allows great openness without sacrifice of stability.

Exterior. Walls: cream stucco. Roof: gravel surfaced capsheet. Trim: salmon colored redwood. Sash and doors salmon sugar pine. Blinds: natural white cedar. Celotex insulation.

Interior. Woodwork: white pine. Living room-dining room ceiling continues through windows to form overhang. Suspended plaster panel 14' wide over fireplace conceals outlets of air-conditioning equipment, circulating fireplace heater grills, and lights.

Cost. $6,970, including 12' x 22' swimming pool, large paved areas for terraces, outdoor barbecue, semi-airconditioning.

Special Features. All rooms have 8' wide doorways to individual gardens. Living room has two 8' sliding doors, giving a 16' opening. Roof overhang of bedroom continues into pergola which crosses pool. The smaller bedroom used as a guest room can be shut off from main part of house.

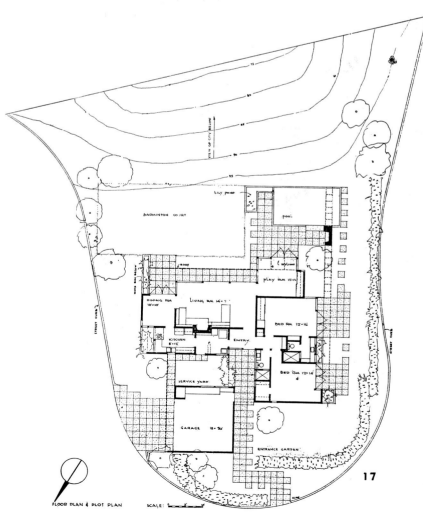

FLOOR PLAN & PLOT PLAN   SCALE:

All Photos: Julius Shulman

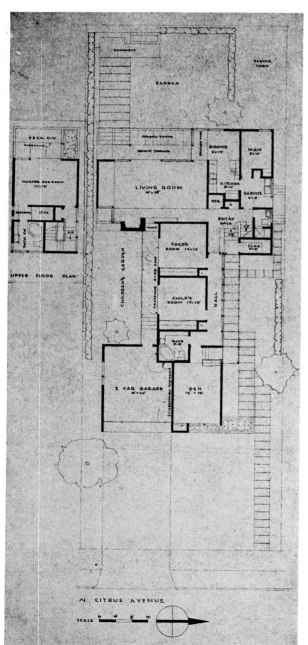

HOUSE FOR A. O. BECKMAN, LOS ANGELES, 1938

Family Composition and Requirements. Family of two adults and two babies; one maid. Provision of seven generous-sized rooms, all with gardens, complete privacy from street and neighbors, on a small inside lot—50' x 135'. Only one room (parents') to be on an upper floor; to provide a den with separate entry, that could be used for a while by children's nurse. All rooms to be accessible from central entry. Living room garden to be separated from children's rooms, but view of children's garden from living room desired.

Site. Level lot. Tract restrictions required that house "face" the street. Opening the den windows toward street was accepted as compliance with this ruling. However, the den also has clerestory windows over garage.

Construction. Post framing, 4" x 4" posts, 4' o.c. (except 8' on centers in living room glass wall). Solid diagonal sheathing under stucco. Cement hearth runs full length of living room, from cement entry floor (on level of exterior cement walk) to cement landing overlooking children's patio.

Exterior. Living room and bedrooms open out on paved terraces at floor level. Parents' bedroom on second floor has a large planted balcony—pergola over.

Interior. Children's rooms have wood paneled walls. Entire south walls of glass, partly in the form of clerestory transoms over a 4' roof canopy. Windows in passage are over entrance walk canopy, for privacy.

Cost. $9,250, including water softener, built-in bookcases and paneled alcove.

GREGORY AIN, Designer
VISSCHER BOYD, Associate

All Photos: Julius Shulman

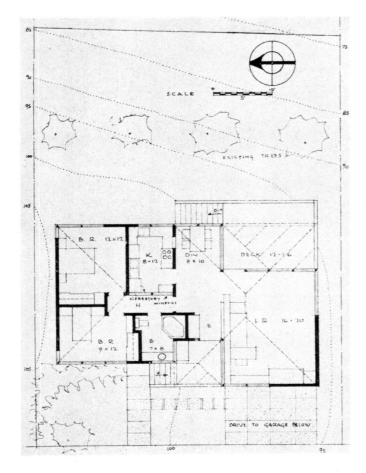

GREGORY AIN, Designer
GEORGE AGRON, Associate

HOUSE FOR URCEL DANIEL, LOS ANGELES, 1939

Family Composition. Young single woman.

Site. Extremely steep, on filled ground.

Construction. Rigidly braced 4" x 4" posts, 4' on centers. Stucco on metal lath.

Exterior. Stucco. Main windows do not face street or adjacent property. Large window on south looks over adjacent lot, considerably lower.

Interior. Walls: natural finish white pine plywood. 4' unit system for use of insulite ceilings. Drawers and cupboards in kitchen open also into dinette. Concealed lights in top of bookcase, which is 16' long screening entry from living room.

Cost. $4,900, including cost of 18'-20' concrete caisson foundation down to solid ground.

Special Features. "Tract restrictions demanded a sloping roof, which was exposed inside. The hollow hipped shell (ceiling) includes pergolas over entry porch and living room deck."

All Photos: George H. Davis Studio, and Haskell

Overhang of roof shades large window in summer. Car port under lower roof at right. Trellis for wistaria, to tie house to land by green foliage wall. Fieldstone wall separates forecourt from sunny south garden. Shade garden in woods on west (rear).

HOUSE FOR MR. AND MRS. WALTER F. BOGNER, LINCOLN, 1939

Family Composition and Requirements. Home for architect, wife and child. Built also as research problem on structural and esthetic problems of modern architecture.

Site. Privacy assured on south and west. Woods on west shade windows in summer. Birch trees featured in views from interior.

Construction. Balloon frame on modular basis of 3'-3½' openings. Fir boarding on exterior. One large plate glass window. Plywood under floors with carpet or linoleum finish. Steel sash. Completely dry-constructed (except foundation and chimney). Designed for standard wallboard sizes.

Exterior. Vertical fir boarding, treated with specially developed penetrating preservative.

Interior. Absence of apparent joint between wallboards in principal rooms accomplished by placing of fenestration and large sheets of wallboard; taped ceiling joints. All wallboard glued, no battens used thus giving effect of solidity usually only obtainable in plaster.

Special Features. Effort to extend modern open planning to a fresher variety of spatial effect, not only bringing in sun and landscape, but also providing enclosed areas to fit varying moods. House framed with continuous floor beams, resting on dropped girts which do not show on inside due to variation of room heights or concealing in closets. All plumbing fixtures on one wall. Absence of floor lamps or lighting fixtures in principal rooms. Designed for minimum cost per room and maximum utilization of amenities of site, using modern architecture as a freedom from patterns to bring garden into house and provide second floor garden terrace. Flexible use of building by combining guest room with owner's sitting room. Laundry combined with maid's bath, providing another multi-purpose room.

(See page 23)

Table designed by architect to seat 8 persons, overcoming problems of grouping couples. Kitchen wall back of table insulated against sound penetration by extra layer of masonite presdwood glued to a layer of homosote.

Alcove designed as "cozy" reading and conversational area, with fireplace at ideal distance from sofa. Lighting (both natural and artificial) eliminates reflections and eyestrain. Fluorescent reading lights under bottom bookshelf provide artificial light equal to natural.

Dining space window, showing modular construction which extends throughout wall surfaces whether glazed or solid. Venetian blinds in pockets.

Ventilation at bottom of window to mix fresh air with preheated airconditioning system. Curtain of heat prevents drafts from glass area and protects plants on stone plant shelf. Window extends above ceiling to add to sense of openness to landscape, providing also concealed curtain rods and venetian blinds.

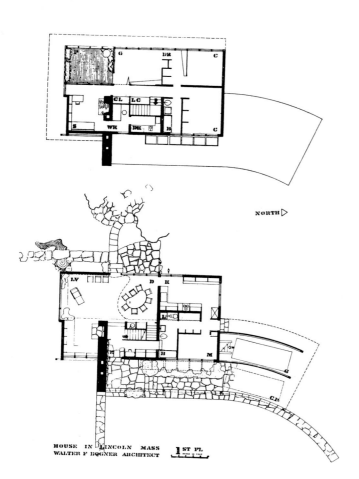

NORTH ▷

HOUSE IN LINCOLN MASS
WALTER F BOGNER ARCHITECT   1 ST FL.

GEORGE W. W. BREWSTER, Jr., Architect

MASSACHUSETTS

Courtesy Architectural Forum

HOUSE FOR MR. AND MRS. EDWARD DANE, ROWLEY, 1938

Family Composition. Man, wife, children, two servants.

Site. On north side of "Long Hill." House is placed along existing private road. Since it is primarily a summer residence the clients wished to favor the view which is to the north, rather than the southerly exposure. Dining room oriented for morning sun; living room for sun all day.

Construction. Wood frame. 2 x 4 studs, clapboards, wood sheathing inside.

Exterior. Main block of house is barn red; one-story wing dark brown; both have white trim at windows and doors.

Interior. Entire house finished in wood. Living and dining rooms sheathed in wide birch boards. The former, including hall, has grey blue ceiling; the latter, dull vermilion. Bathrooms plastered and painted. Service portions have painted plywood walls; the rest of house has pine sheathing, stained and waxed.

Cost. 37¢ per cubic foot including all casework in kitchen and pantry, bookcase in living room. Economical feature is central bearing partition.

Deliberate use has been made of traditional New England exterior finish to harmonize with farm houses of vicinity.

Living room showing vertical birch sheathing and windows to south.

FIRST FLOOR

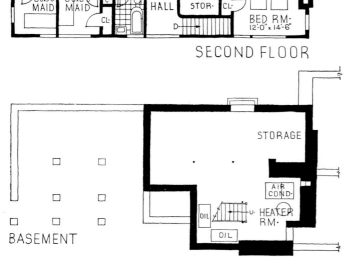

SECOND FLOOR

BASEMENT

HOUSE FOR MR. AND MRS. LAURENCE H. H. JOHNSON, JR., MARBLEHEAD, 1937

Family Composition. Man, wife, two children, two servants. House primarily for summer use.

Site. Lot on a point at ocean's edge. Plan is result of effort to have all rooms face view, sun, and prevailing breezes, and to create as much privacy within and in front of house as possible. Problem complicated by unusual shape of lot, the fact that it sloped uphill to the sea-wall, and the existence of a house to the east three feet from lot line.

Construction. Wood frame, balloon type. 2 x 6 studs, clapboards and plaster.

Exterior. Painted grey with white chimney, fences, etc. Slate roof (which was a definite requirement) is black.

Interior. All interiors painted flat colors.

Cost. 55¢ per cubic foot including casework in pantry and kitchen, and bookcase in study.

Orientation for sunlight, view and privacy. A successful attempt to adapt Colonial to more modern lines. Terraces planned as integral part of the design.

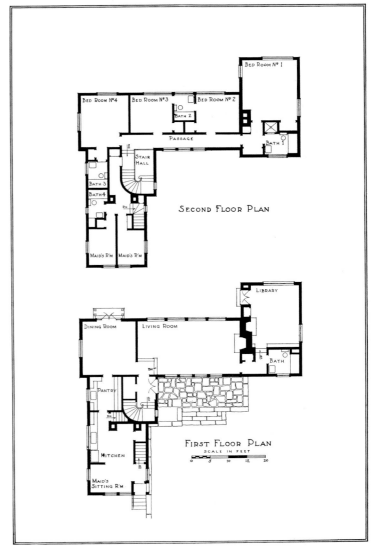

SECOND FLOOR PLAN

FIRST FLOOR PLAN

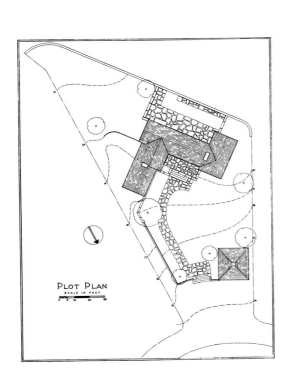

PLOT PLAN

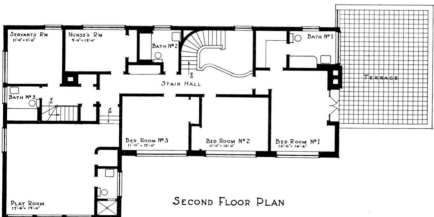

SECOND FLOOR PLAN

Servants R'm 11'-0" × 15'-0"
Nurse's R'm 9'-0" × 12'-0"
Bath Nº 2
Bath Nº 1
Bath Nº 3
Stair Hall
Terrace
Bed Room Nº 3 11'-0" × 15'-0"
Bed Room Nº 2 11'-0" × 13'-0"
Bed Room Nº 1 12'-6" × 14'-6"
Play Room 17'-6" × 19'-0"

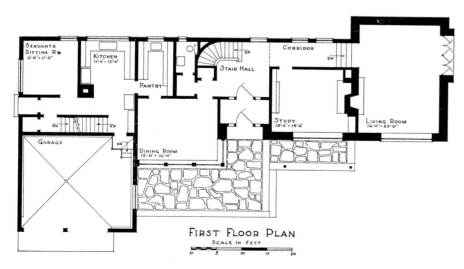

FIRST FLOOR PLAN
SCALE IN FEET
0   5   10   15   20

Servants Sitting R'm 11'-0" × 11'-0"
Kitchen 11'-0" × 15'-0"
Pantry
Stair Hall
Corridor
Study 13'-0" × 14'-6"
Living Room 16'-0" × 22'-0"
Garage
Dining Room 12'-6" × 16'-0"

GEORGE W. W. BREWSTER, Jr., Architect

HOUSE FOR MR. AND MRS. GREELY CURTIS, JR., BELMONT, 1937

Family Composition. Man, wife, children, two servants.

Site. Lot situated near top of Belmont Hill with view east and southeast over Boston to the ocean. Design and placing of house result of attempt to (1) give all rooms southerly exposure; (2) take advantage of view; (3) provide as much play space as possible; and (4) make house private regardless of future development of adjacent lots.

Construction. Wood frame balloon type. 2 x 6 studs, clapboards and plaster. Prefabricated wood and metal parts to a varying degree. Copper shield on top of all masonry walls as protection against termites.

Exterior. Choice of materials and finish influenced by desire to accentuate the peculiarly local aspects of the house.

Interior. Most of the walls painted in flat colors. The color scheme starts with wallpaper on end wall only of living room, which is dark green with a grey, white and terra cotta design. The ceiling is terra cotta, the walls grey or white. The blues, tans, yellow, grey or white used elsewhere are meant to be consistent.

Cost. 53¢ per cubic foot including all casework in pantry and kitchen, bookcases and cabinets in study.

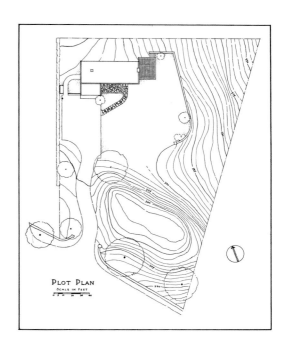

PLOT PLAN
SCALE IN FEET

KENNETH DAY, Architect

All Photos: C. V. D. Hubbard　　　　　　　　　　　　　　　Courtesy *Architectural Record*

HOUSE FOR MARSHALL COLE, NEW HOPE, 1936

Family Composition. Husband, manufacturer of textiles; wife, painter; two small children. Wanted efficient plan and mechanical plant so house could be run with no servant or with one or two.

Site. Site of old limekilns; old stone available. Terrain artificial but covered with old trees and moss.

Construction. Basement stone with precast joist and slab construction. Superstructure frame. Old stone from limekilns; exterior above unfinished T & G cypress boards. Prefabricated parts: concrete joists; integral screen steel casement windows.

Interior. Insulating boards unfinished 4′ x 12′, and painted masonite board in bathrooms. Woodwork natural red beech. Ground floor concrete finished in terra cotta metalichron finish. Neutral plaster walls and ceilings.

Cost. $20,000, including built-in furniture and lighting. Special economy in planning: only corridor space is one stair hall providing access to two maids' rooms as well as usual list of owner's, guest, and children's rooms.

Sliding panels of glass, behind the day bed, separate work area from sleeping area.

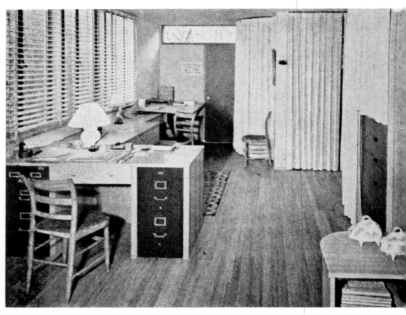

Work area contains many examples of furniture built in to fit the owner's requirements.

DECK

B.
B.

BED ROOM
13'-9" x 13'-10"

BED ROOM
13'-8" 19'-1"

L.

D   D

B

BED ROOM
10'-4" x 20'-3"

GLASS
PANEL

DRESSING
ROOM

DECK

U

SECOND FLOOR

D   D

BATH

SLEEPING

DRESSING

OWNER'S SLEEPING AREA

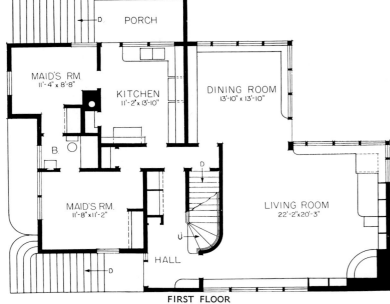

PORCH

D

MAID'S RM.
11'-4" x 8'-8"

KITCHEN
11'-2" x 13'-10"

DINING ROOM
13'-10" x 13'-10"

B.

D

MAID'S RM.
11'-8" x 11'-2"

LIVING ROOM
22'-2" x 20'-3"

U

HALL

D

FIRST FLOOR

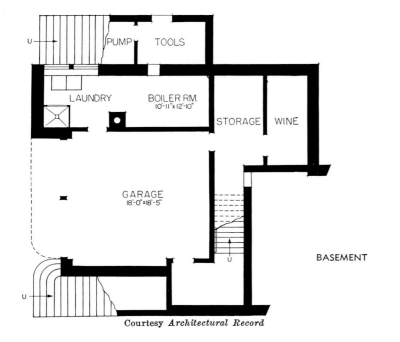

U

PUMP   TOOLS

LAUNDRY

BOILER RM.
10'-11" x 12'-10"

STORAGE   WINE

GARAGE
18'-0" x 18'-5"

U

BASEMENT

U

Courtesy *Architectural Record*

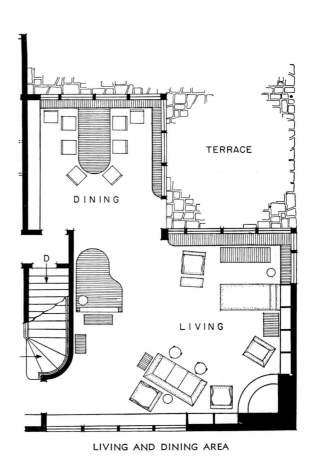

TERRACE

DINING

D

LIVING

LIVING AND DINING AREA

Cypress siding and walls of old stone against background of native trees.

House for Marshall Cole, New Hope, 1936 (continued).

Courtesy *Architectural Record*

Photo: *Robert M. Damora*   Courtesy *Architectural Forum*

HOUSE FOR KENNETH DAY, MIQUON, 1937

Family Composition. Man, wife, three children under fifteen.

Site. One of three new houses to be placed on a high field with commanding view southeast, south, and southwest.

Construction. Concrete floors, masonry walls. Stone foundations, steel sash. Prefabricated parts: stock steel sash; prefabricated concrete joists. Propane gas serving three houses for all equipment from one tank.

Exterior. Painted cinder blocks. Poured concrete finished deck floor.

Interior. Varnished masonite dadoes. Unfinished insulating board above dadoes. Lacquered copper over master's bathtub. Terra cotta colored metalichron finished floors; coloring for finished floors sanded directly on damp monolithic concrete.

Cost. Approximately $21,500, including built-in furniture and built-in lighting. Special economy consisted of building three houses of different designs but similar materials under one contract. Also direct use of color in floor slabs, and open beam treatment of concrete ceilings produced fireproof house at only slight cost above non-fireproof house.

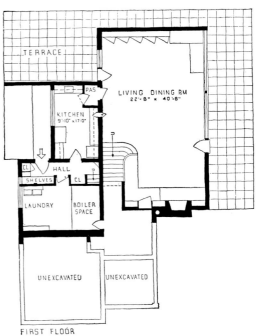

FIRST FLOOR

SECOND FLOOR

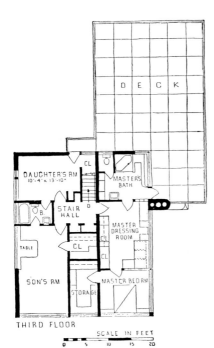

THIRD FLOOR

SCALE IN FEET
0   5   10   15   20

All Photos: Hedrich-Blessing Studio

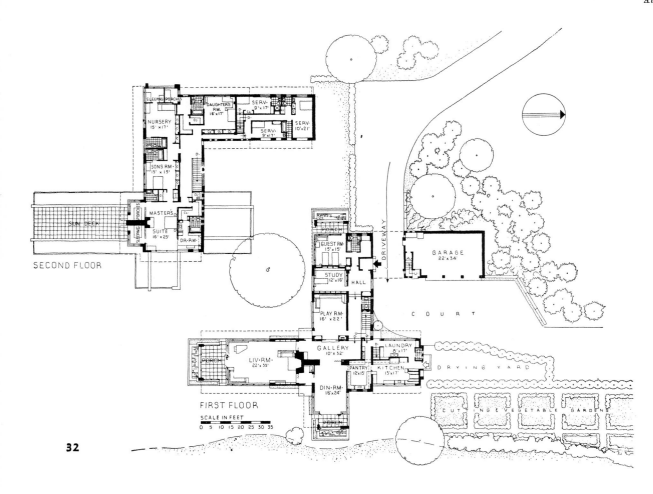

SECOND FLOOR

FIRST FLOOR
SCALE IN FEET
0 5 10 15 20 25 30 35

Courtesy *Architectural Forum*

HOUSE FOR WALTER J. KOHLER, JR., KOHLER, 1937

Family Composition and Requirements. Husband, wife, three children and three servants. Sharp separation of family life from reception end of house desired. Children to have their own living room apart from parents and yet close to service rooms.

Site. House placed on the edge of a bluff which drops about 40 feet to the east. Fifty-four acres of pasture and woodland. House commands view of valley to the east and south. To the west a rise shelters house from highway.

Construction. Steel and concrete frame from which wood roof slabs and floors are suspended. Concrete encased steel beams are exposed above the roof. Walls, except on north, are 4" brick and 4" tile serving merely as a curtain filler. North wall is a bearing wall of masonry. Suspended roof construction designed to ensure level ceiling with windows rising full height of wall.

Exterior. All wood used on exterior Tidewater red cypress. Brick "tan colonial" laid with header course depressed about ½". Tar and gravel roof laid level and designed to carry 2" of water for insulation in summer.

Interior. Ceilings and most of the walls sand-floated plaster integrally colored. Chimney and other bearing points of same brick masonry as exterior. Wood in principal rooms on first floor selected red birch and in bedrooms selected white birch. Floors white maple except in hallways and stairs which are reinforced concrete covered with linoleum in inlaid patterns.

Cost. 64¢ per cubic foot, including built-in furniture and cabinet work. Planning of furniture and furnishings along with design of house permitted omission of plastering on walls where furniture was to be placed.

Entrance side on north

Courtesy *Architectural Forum*   Photo: *Parker-Griffith*

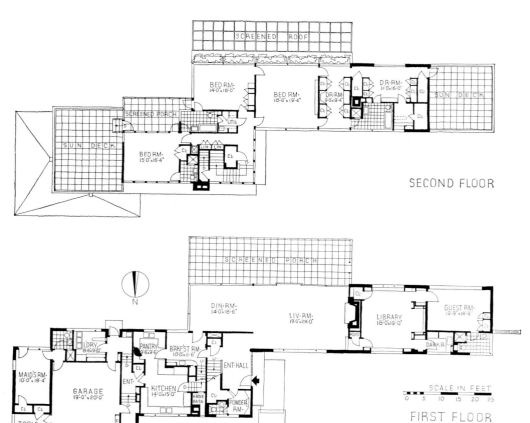

SECOND FLOOR

FIRST FLOOR

SCALE IN FEET
0   5   10   15   20   25

HOUSE FOR H. STANLEY MARCUS, DALLAS, 1937

Family Composition and Requirements. Family of three. Interested in health and social activities. Large collections of books and prints.

Site. View and shape of terrain determined orientation and therefore the plan.

Construction. Brick and redwood. Roof: 20-year bonded tar and gravel. Floors: concrete slab on fill. Insulation: walls, metallation; roof, metallation and rock wool. Glass: double strength, quality A; 3/16 in. plate for doors. Hot air heating equipped with humidity apparatus and automatic humidifying and temperature control; forced air furnace with ducts insulated for future cooling.

Exterior. Brick veneer and redwood. Two sundecks. All exterior redwood varnished to preserve color. Steel sash. Overhangs for shade. Terrace screened overhead and equipped with awning which is rolled up into recess at night.

Interior. Redwood ceilings in living room, dining room, and hall. Library all redwood. Walls are sheetrock covered with decorators' canvas, which permits elimination of all trim. Floor coverings: living room, library, dining and breakfast room of ½ in. cork; kitchen, linoleum; bathrooms, rubber. Doors: birch veneer and redwood. Cabinets: magnolia and quartered oak. Concealed lights in trough in living room and hall.

Photo: Elmer L. Astleford

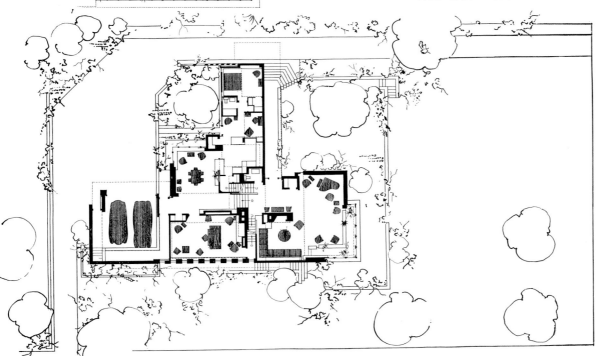

HOUSE FOR MR. AND MRS. JAMES T. PARDEE, MIDLAND, 1937

Family Composition. Family of two, with maids' quarters and guest room.

Site. Taking advantage of river view as seen from living room window and park view from bedrooms.

Construction. Patented Dow cinder blocks; concrete floors throughout, with upper floors of concrete over wire lath on steel joists. Poured reinforced concrete foundation. Gas-fired split system for heating. 4" insulation on all ceilings and stud walls exposed to exterior.

Exterior. Cinder blocks with white waterproof covering. Steel sash throughout, with copper spandrels, patina finish. Flat roof of built-up bonded roofings. Louisiana red cypress trim. Planted terrace surrounded by cinder block wall. Electrically operated garage door; control from dash of car.

Interior. Walls and ceilings are all white. Bathrooms have tile walls and floors. Floors: basement, cement finish; kitchen, service wing and game room, cork tile; remainder of house, brilliant green carpet.

Cost. 67¢ per cubic foot.

All Photos: W. Boychuk

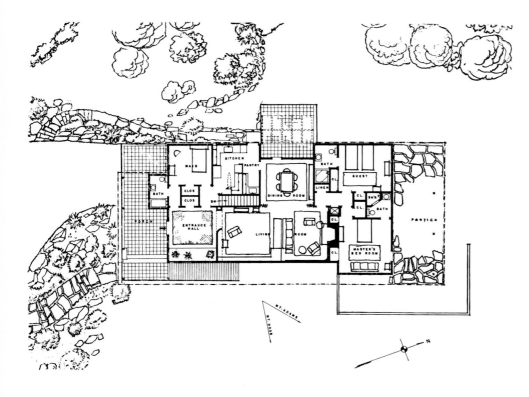

HOUSE FOR JENNINGS F. SUTOR, PORTLAND, 1938

Family Composition. Bachelor who entertains often.

Site. Hillside property commanding view. Background of tall firs and cedars.

Construction. Frame on concrete foundation walls.

Interior. Finished in white sand-floated plaster. A large section over and around fireplace is covered with zebra flexwood. Ceiling of entry hall made of woven fir slats 1/8″ thick and 2½″ wide. Floor covering is straw matting from South Sea Islands. The rest of the oak floors have large light apple green rugs. Wall between entry and living room covered with gold Japanese straw paper to form background for a Chinese painting. One wall of entry hall has large vertical grain fir panels left natural in color.

Cost. About $15,000 without landscaping.

A. E. DOYLE & ASSOCIATE, Architects
P. BELLUSCHI, Designing Architect

Courtesy
Architectural Record

A. E. DOYLE & ASSOCIATE, Architects
P. BELLUSCHI, Designing Architect

Photo: W. Boychuk   Courtesy *Architectural Record*

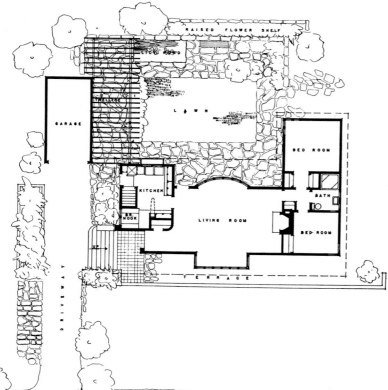

HOUSE FOR MR. AND MRS. PIETRO BELLUSCHI, PORTLAND, 1937

Family Composition and Requirements. Young couple of moderate means and limited social activities. Garden an important consideration.

Site. Only problem of site was to preserve view of valley and to create a level lawn at rear to serve as outdoor living place sheltered from intruders.

Construction. Frame on concrete foundation walls. Materials: wood, split tiles, and plaster. Brick, 12" long, 4" wide, and 1" thick obtained by scoring a 4" x 4" hollow tile in such a way that each tile gives four bricks.

Exterior. All materials left as much as possible with their natural color. Fenestration grouped in few large windows so that maximum amount of wall space be left for furniture. Roof kept fairly flat at eaves to give a feeling of lightness; it is steeper over the house proper. Architect felt that overhanging eaves are convenient in a climate where rains and winds are prevalent for many months of year; also that if enough glass is provided for light and view the overhanging eve gives protection from glare and direct sunshine, and helps to strengthen the feeling of shelter.

Interior. Living room in smooth plaster with casein paint; fireplace polished marble. One partition covered in figured walnut flexwood. Softwood floor covered with mustard colored carpet. Bedroom has oak floors and Japanese straw paper on walls. Studio has fir wall panelling. Kitchen painted light ivory, with black linoleum floor and counter tops.

Cost. About $5,000 including dishwashing and garbage disposal unit, air conditioning unit, plumbing fixtures, gas hot water heater, wiring, light fixtures, thermax insulation, etc.

PHILIP L. GOODWIN, Architect

All Photos: T. P. Robinson

HOUSE FOR JAMES L. GOODWIN IN WINTER PARK, 1939

Family Composition and Requirements. Two adults. No children. All service from nearby hotel. Winter resort for health reasons.

Site. View of lake. Sixty-foot pines.

Construction. Cinder block with white stucco. Prefabricated parts: glass brick; large glass windows.

Exterior. Rather flat roof of Ludowici tile to avoid boxy feeling disliked by owner. Strong horizontal lines.

Interior. Living room and porch form a more or less open single space, with minimum of interference for large parties, and with views of lake.

Cost. $25,000 including glazed bookshelves, cupboards, radio, telephone, all kitchen equipment and closets, heating, etc.

All Photos: T. P. Robinson

House for James L. Goodwin, Winter Park, 1939 (continued).

Cinder block walls with white stucco, and overhanging tiled roof.

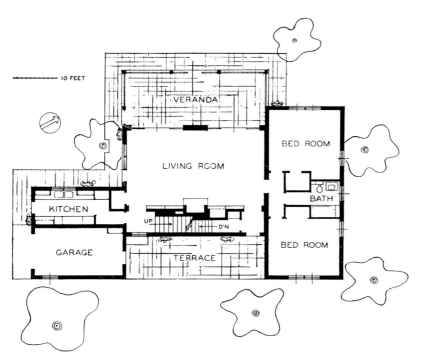

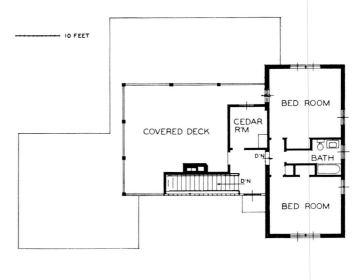

WALTER GROPIUS and MARCEL BREUER,
Associated Architects

All Photos: Paul Davis, George H. Davis Studio

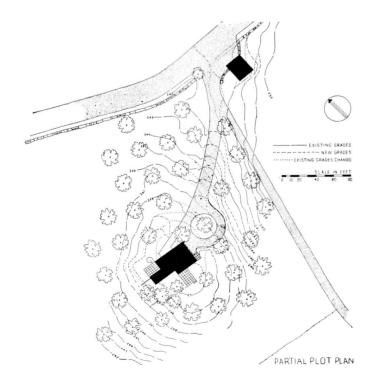

EXISTING GRADES
NEW GRADES
EXISTING GRADES CHANGED

SCALE IN FEET
0 10 20   40   60   80

PARTIAL PLOT PLAN

HOUSE FOR MR. AND MRS. WALTER GROPIUS, LINCOLN, 1938

Family Composition. Two adults, one child, one maid.

Site. Best views towards south and west.

Construction. Redwood sheathing, painted white. Cabot's quilt insulation. Tile and gravel roofs. Hope's windows, heavy sash.

Exterior. Roof overhang on southern side of house protects living and dining room from sun during hot summer months, but permits the lower winter sun to penetrate these rooms.

Interior. Living room, dining room, study have California acoustical plaster over all ceilings and walls. Walls of hall covered with normal clapboards fixed vertically. No corridor; all rooms having access from central hall.

Special Comments. Design deliberately tries to fit into the order of white Colonial houses in the vicinity without imitating them. The main type of construction, the exterior sheathing and the white paint indicate some of these connections.

Courtesy *Architectural Forum*

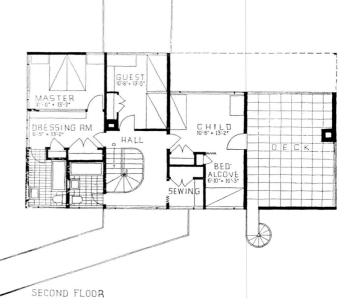

SECOND FLOOR

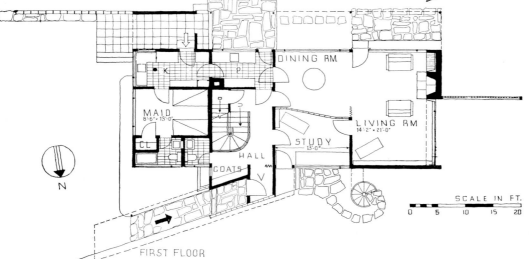

FIRST FLOOR

SCALE IN FT.
0   5   10   15   20

N

WALTER GROPIUS and MARCEL BREUER,
Associated Architects

All Photos: Paul Davis, George H. Davis Studio

House for Mr. and Mrs. Walter Gropius, Lincoln, 1938 (continued).

Courtesy Architectural Forum

WALTER GROPIUS and MARCEL BREUER,
Associated Architects

All Photos: George H. Davis Studio

HOUSE FOR MRS. JOSEPHINE HAGERTY, COHASSET, 1938

Family Composition. Mother and three adult sons.

Site. Beach, on a projecting point overlooking Atlantic Ocean.

Construction. Combination steel and wood frame; rubble stone.

Exterior. Exterior stairs: cypress treads on welded and galvanized pipe frame. Service stairs: precast concrete slabs cantilevered from stone wall. Wood roof deck covering. Concrete terrace under house. All rubble stone from site.

Interior. Oak floors, plaster walls and ceilings. Interior stair: oak treads on welded pipe frame. Natural color wood sheathing in stair hall. Large sliding glass door between living room and porch.

SECOND FLOOR

1 stair hall	7 bed room
2 corridor	8 bed room
3 master b.r.	9 bath
4 bed room	10 bed room
5 terrace	11 terrace
6 bath	

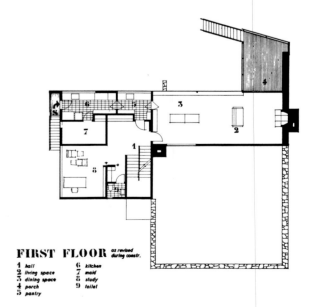

FIRST FLOOR *as revised during constr.*

1 hall	6 kitchen
2 living space	7 maid
3 dining space	8 study
4 porch	9 toilet
5 pantry	

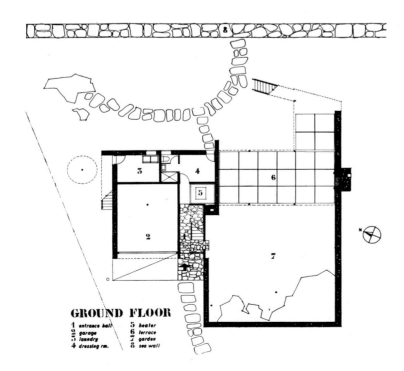

GROUND FLOOR

1 entrance hall	5 heater
2 garage	6 terrace
3 laundry	7 garden
4 dressing rm.	8 sea wall

WALTER GROPIUS and MARCEL BREUER,
Associated Architects

Entrance, with east exposure.

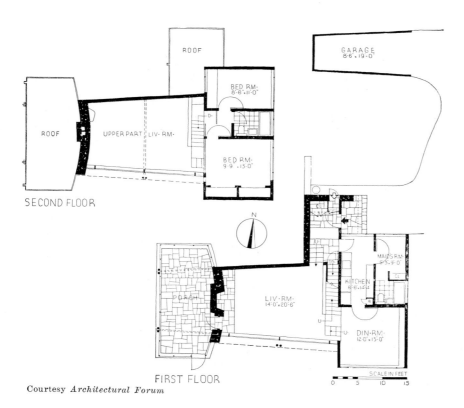

SECOND FLOOR

FIRST FLOOR

Courtesy *Architectural Forum*

HOUSE FOR MARCEL BREUER, LINCOLN, 1939

Site. Front (east part) level; back slopes. House located on edge of slope. South wall of living room is on a true east-west line.

Construction. Wood frame. Dry construction throughout. Steel sash, casement type. Metal kitchen cabinets. Columns: hard pine. Structure: fir. Masonite window panels.

Exterior. Vertical T & G redwood. No gutters or conductors. Stone floor in porch.

Interior. Stone floor in entry. Kitchen and bathrooms linoleum floors; carpet elsewhere. Screens: penoleum in wood frames. Walls and ceilings: plywood panels; some walls ¼ sawed fir.

Two-story living room facing south.

Porch, screened in, facing due west.

Courtesy *Architectural Forum*   *All Photos: Ezra Stoller*

All Photos: Ezra Stoller

House for Marcel Breuer, Lincoln, 1939 (continued).

Corner of living room, looking into dining room below and study-bedroom above.

WALTER GROPIUS and MARCEL BREUER,
Associated Architects

Photo: *Haskell*

HOUSE FOR MR. AND MRS. JAMES FORD, LINCOLN, 1939

Family Composition and Requirements. Two adults, daughter, and maid. Privacy for work, economy of construction, ease of maintenance.

Site. In orchard at edge of extensive woods. Orientation for sunlight and view.

Construction. Wood frame; vertical siding. Foundation of 12″ concrete blocks. Prefabricated parts: 4′ x 8′ weldboard plywood panelling for all walls and ceilings, except in service area and bathrooms where plaster was used. Windows: metal casement. Sun screen for entire length of second story, made of redwood boards on specially designed galvanized brackets; to exclude sun's rays in summer. Four bathrooms on one stack. Heater and two fireplaces on one chimney.

Exterior. White painted sheathing. Copper termite proofing and flashing. Tar and gravel roof. Terrace wall of granite. Flagstone terrace.

Interior. Vertical clapboards in hall, painted white. End wall of staircase, canyon red. Weldboard walls and ceilings painted grey in living and dining rooms and on two sides of master bedroom; two walls of master bedroom soft peach; blue in daughter's room; white in halls and study. Carpeted floors in living room, dining room, and master bedroom. Black linoleum in halls and bathrooms; grey linoleum in study, kitchen, and maid's room. Hardware, chrome finish. Glass partition over buffet between living room and dining room; also between dressing room and bedroom. Metal kitchen cabinets, in all-electric kitchen. Built-in bookcases and cabinets in study and living room.

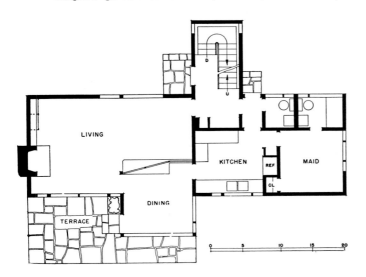

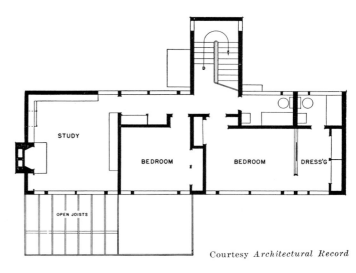

Courtesy *Architectural Record*

All Photos: Haskell

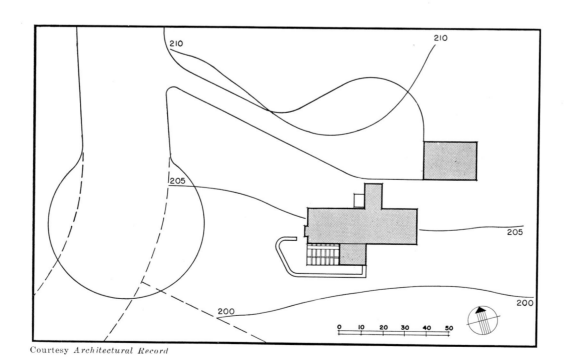

Courtesy Architectural Record

House for Mr. and Mrs. James
Ford, Lincoln, 1939 (continued).

WALTER GROPIUS and MARCEL BREUER,
Associated Architects

All Photos: Haskell

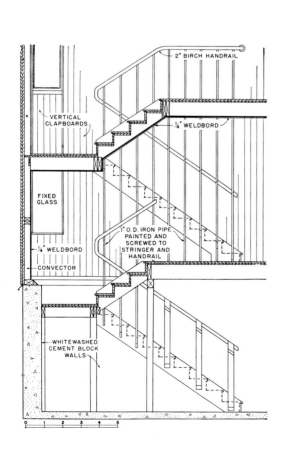

2" BIRCH HANDRAIL

VERTICAL
CLAPBOARDS

¼" WELDBORD

FIXED
GLASS

1" O.D. IRON PIPE
PAINTED AND
SCREWED TO
STRINGER AND
HANDRAIL

¼" WELDBORD

CONVECTOR

WHITEWASHED
CEMENT BLOCK
WALLS

Courtesy Architectural Record

All Photos: Fred R. Dapprich

Sixty-four feet of sliding glass panels folding screenlike beneath a simple roof, open the house into the garden.

Courtesy *Architectural Forum*

CALIFORNIA

HARWELL HAMILTON HARRIS, Designer

HOUSE FOR GEORGE C. BAUER, GLENDALE, 1938

Family Composition and Requirements. Three adults, two children. Family life and care of children chief considerations.

Site. Level lot 65' wide, facing north.

Exterior. Wood frame. Stucco. Garden wall of vertical redwood boards. Terraces cement blocks cast in place.

Interior. Walls integrally colored stucco. Most of lighting built in. Kitchen and bathroom floors linoleum; all others covered with Chinese grass matting, which is inexpensive, easy to clean, sound absorbent and rich in appearance. Curtains: natural color pongee. Doors and windows slide horizontally on bottom track. Economies consist largely of built-in features: couch, bookcase, wood box, dressing table, chest of drawers, beds and cabinet.

Special Comments. Since both privacy and sunlight are at back and east of lot, the house becomes an "L" which screens garden from street and neighbors. All principal rooms open on garden, the other two walls of which are tree-covered hill slopes. Some rooms are turned 45° to shorten halls or rooms, open the approach, avoid a tree or allow the garden to penetrate the mass of the house. Children's bedrooms are provided with wide openings to each other and to sunny playroom opening on a garden. Service yard on street side gives greater privacy to rear garden and insulates house from street.

Courtesy *Architectural Forum*

Lightness, openness, natural colors and
scale were considered important.

All Photos: Fred R. Dapprich

HOUSE IN FELLOWSHIP PARK, LOS ANGELES, 1936

Family Composition and Requirements.
Two adults, both employed, who pre-
ferred simple accommodations to a mort-
gage.

Site. Due to beauty of site, dwelling
was planned to appear as a mere incident
in the landscape.

Construction. Continuous built-up girders at floor and ceiling, and continuous
posts on isolated footings, braced by
compression-tension buttresses, make up
the skeleton of this light-weight structure. Materials used are redwood, celotex, masonite hardboard and glass, with
some tile and rubber in kitchen and
bathroom.

Interior. With the exception of narrow
frames of windows, which are dyed black,
all wood is left natural. In living room,
redwood wall, celotex ceilings, white pine
lighting cornice and straw matting floors
are left natural.

Cost. Approximately $3.50 per square
foot.

Special Comments. "Harmony with the
rocks and foliage was sought, so floor,
roof, terrace and other large planes are
given uniform pattern and texture. By
designing the house on a three-foot unit,
every opening, every wall space is kept a
multiple of three feet. This gives a
rhythm to the design which is felt even
when it is not consciously perceived, and
provides an air of restfulness."

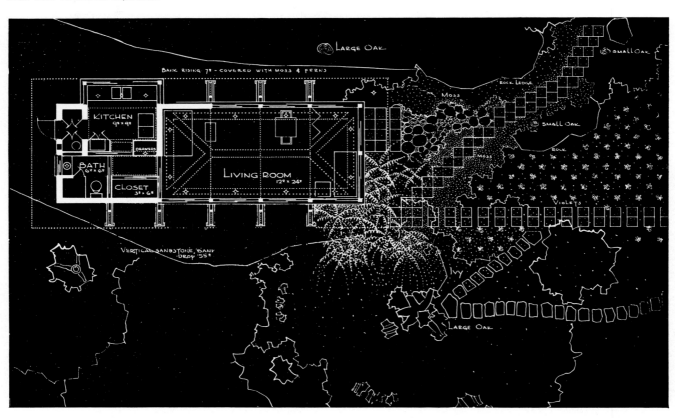

To harmonize with natural materials in living room, richness of color was used in bathroom and kitchen. Thus drainboard, backsplash and floor are a deep blue, window frames black, walls pale vermilion, open shelves deep vermilion, upper walls and ceiling mustard yellow. Instead of cupboards above counter space there is a small ventilated pantry for food storage. This gives more room than the usual arrangement, makes only one door to open, and allows windows to be placed all around the sink. The windows are removable and in summer can be taken out, leaving only the screens.

Rails of the sliding panels are dyed black and further accent is furnished by dark teak furniture, a gold leaf screen, dark blue cushions, and a blue and vermilion embroidered couch cover.

City house of local conventional materials.

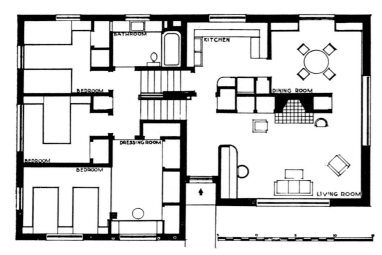

HOUSE FOR MR. AND MRS. CHAPMAN YOUNG, JR., DENVER, 1937

Family Composition. Young couple and baby; part-time servant.

Site. Access from street only. High ground.

Construction. Conventional solid masonry walls, wood joists. Buff face brick and lumber. Prefabricated parts: wallboard panels.

Exterior. Roof deck exposed south and west, screened from neighbors on east. Buff face brick, red trim.

Interior. No plaster except in garage and on chimney breast. Upper level interiors all furred with wallboard. Brick exposed downstairs.

Cost. $9,800 including all built-in furniture, fixtures and furnace.

Special Comments. Minimum steps between levels; minimum circulation; maximum living areas.

Master bedroom from dressing room, showing built-in beds and dressing table.

All Photos: Robert M. Damora

HOUSE IN DELAWARE, 1938

Requirements. Especial attention given to orientation, view, approach, deck or outdoor living requirements with the necessary privacy, convenience of service, minimum upkeep costs, gracious living rooms both for intimate living and entertaining. Desire of owner for a direct connection between master's garage and study without going by the service quarters made a separate garage necessary for the servants.

Site. A large acreage of rolling open fields with woods north of house and a view to south.

Construction. Fire-resisting. Steel, concrete, and brick.

Exterior. Stainless steel window sills with steel casements. Roofs: concrete slab of light weight on steel joists with 5 ply built-up roofing. Decks: concrete slabs with slate tile laid in mastic. Terraces: colored concrete. Special hardware both exterior and interior designed by the architects.

Interior. Wall covering: cherry ¾" plywood in study and stair hall dado; birch ¾" plywood in living room and master's dressing room; Carrara glass in bathrooms. Doors: flush birch veneer. Trim and cabinets painted pine. Plaster walls painted in pastel tones with walls catching the light in a cool color and walls not catching the light in a warm color. Floors: masonite interlocking cushion flooring. Special light fixtures designed by architects. Heating and air conditioning: complete Delco system with provision for summer cooling later.

Special Equipment. Radio outlets in each room; garage doors operated electrically from switch in drive; garbage disposal in sink; exhaust fan and hood exhaust over stove.

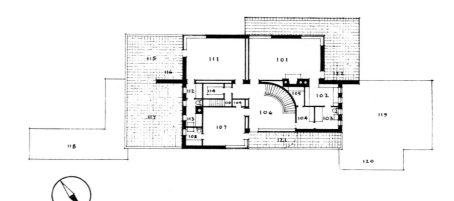

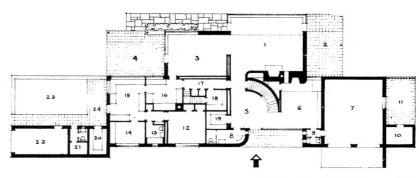

1, Living Room; 2, Living Porch; 3, Dining Room; 4, Dining Porch; 5, Entrance Hall; 6, Study; 7, Garage; 8, Powder Room; 9, Entry and Lavatory; 10, Tools; 11, Garden Porch; 12, Servants Room; 13, Bath; 14, Laundry and Sitting; 15, Kitchen; 16, Pantry; 17, Passage; 18, Storage; 19, Coat Closet; 20, Cold Room; 21, Wood Storage and Lav.; 22, Servants Garage; 23, Service Court; 101, Master's Bedroom; 102, Master's Dressing Room; 103, Master's Bath; 104, Storage; 105, Cedar Closet; 106, Hall; 107, Guest Room; 108, Bath; 109, Closet; 110, Service Stair; 111, Guest Room; 112 Dressing Closet; 113, Bath; 114, Linen; 115, Sundeck; 116, Fin Walls; 117, Shade Deck; 118, Roof; 119, Roof; 120, Cantilever; 121, Deck.

House in Delaware, 1938 (continued).

All Photos: Ben Schnall

HOUSE FOR MRS. CLARA FARGO THOMAS AT SOMES SOUND, MOUNT DESERT, 1939

Requirements. House to be designed entirely for summer use. Present building is a portion of contemplated development. Other buildings, one for owner, another for children and their guests (latter to include a boat-house and float), are to be added later, leaving central structure as a dining and guest house.

Site. Rocky headland between two beaches, facing Somes Sound. Contours and landscape of rocks and native growth left undisturbed even in immediate neighborhood of house, which has been placed with consideration for every natural feature of the site.

Construction. Foundations laid on ledge without excavation. Only grading is that made necessary by the road. Foundation walls: selected field stone. Framing: 6" x 6" posts 10' on centers, with addition of occasional 5' bays, where a 15' dimension required. Intervening studding acts as curtain. Lintels over posts set above ceiling joists, which act also as tie-beams, so that ceiling runs out flush to edge of eaves. Windows: wood sash, largely sliding. Roof: wood shingles.

Exterior. Variegated granite foundations, oiled cedar clapboards, and silver grey shingles, to merge with natural surroundings. Windows and railings painted light grey-umber; underside of eaves pale grey-blue.

Interior. Walls: lined with ¼" plywood, birch in hall-dining room, oak in living room, fir in remainder of house, attached to studs with brass screws and finished with spar varnish. Floors in the same spaces of birch, oak and pine, respectively, unstained and waxed. Plank ceilings and windows painted same color as exterior. Built-in cabinet work matches walls in every case.

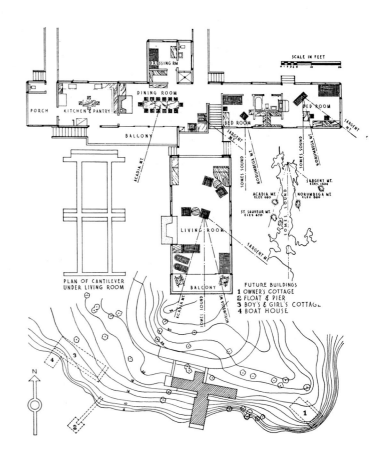

All Photos: Ben Schnall

House for Mrs. Clara Fargo
Thomas at Somes Sound,
Mount Desert 1939
(continued).

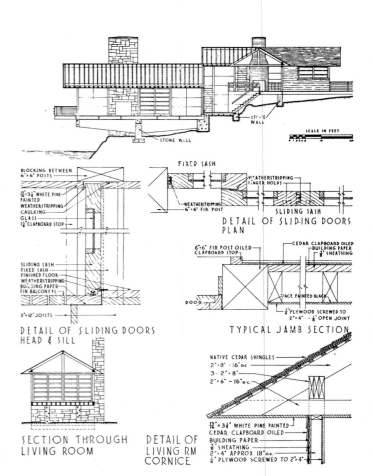

All Photos: Richard T. Dooner

"SQUARE SHADOWS," HOME OF MR. AND MRS. WILLIAM STIX WASSERMAN, NEAR CHESTNUT HILL, 1934

Family Composition and Requirements. Mr. and Mrs. Wasserman and three children. Owners interested in politics, finance, and the arts. Musical and dance recitals frequently given. Active participants in country life and sports.

Plan. "The lines of human circulation on the plans are curvilinear axes of actual movement which replace the old rectangular axes of theoretical movement."

Construction. All bearing walls are of grey local rubble masonry. All curtain walls of light red Virginia brick. Air conditioning.

Interior. Much of the furniture, particularly that in dining rooms, designed by architect. Subtle use of color as background for Oriental painting, sculpture, and screens which decorate the principal rooms. Two dining rooms, one for the children and one for the parents and their guests, both served by a common pantry; when partition between is folded back the entire space becomes available for a large party.

Cost. Approximately $160,000.

Comments. "The use of the handrail of laminated wood as a beam supporting the semi-circular staircase is perhaps a novel structural device."

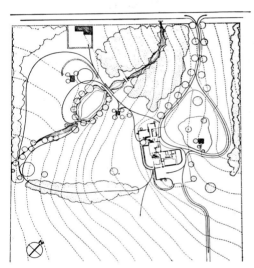

PLOT PLAN

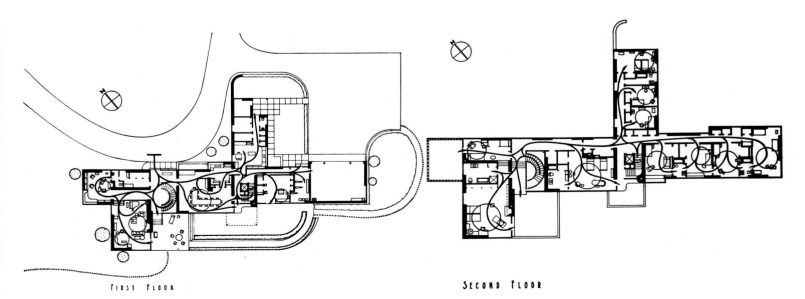

FIRST FLOOR

SECOND FLOOR

House for Mr. and Mrs. William Stix Wasserman, near Chestnut Hill, 1934 (continued).

The stair is supported by its spiral rails composed of laminated wood panels fabricated at the joiner's shop and screwed and bolted together in place. The finished panels of veneered teak wood were also applied in place. The diagonal light and shadow lines of the venetian blinds give an idea of the luminosity produced by glazing both ends of the hall from wall to wall.

Photos: Hedrich-Blessing Studio
Courtesy Architectural Forum

HOUSE FOR MR. AND MRS. ALFRED J. BROMFIELD, JR., DENVER, 1936

Site. View of Rocky Mountain Range to north, west, and south. House situated on westerly sloping hill.

Construction. Brick. Roof: light fir trusses covered with sheathing and ¾" elaterite roofing. Decks: joists, sheathing and canvas topped with elaterite. Insulation for walls and roof, rock wool. Attic and kitchen ventilators. Air-conditioned.

Exterior. Walls: brick and wood lap-siding. Wood painted dark grey-blue; brick, a cool light grey. Joints between glass brick painted grey-green. Entrance door, sharp yellow. Casement windows.

Interior. Floors: fir throughout, covered with linoleum. Walls: living room, linoleum at fireplace; bedrooms, quilted chintz at head of bed; kitchen and bathrooms, linoleum; other walls, plaster. Ceilings and walls painted yellow in living room; light grey in dining room and upstairs sitting room; shades of blue in master bedroom; grey and blue, and grey and green combinations in dressing rooms and servants' rooms.

Cost. $24,633.

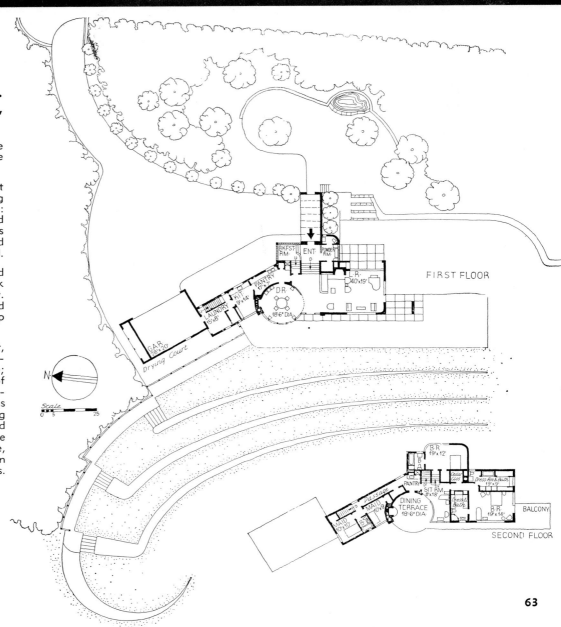

FIRST FLOOR

SECOND FLOOR

All Photos: Hedrich-Blessing Studio   Courtesy *Architectural Record*

HOUSE FOR HERBERT BRUNING, WILMETTE, 1935

Family Composition. Family of five, two boys and girl; servants. Much entertaining at home. Informal way of life.

Site. Restricted area in suburban town.

Construction. Welded. Structural steel frame; non-bearing walls and partitions. Column centers equal both directions. Flat roof to carry water; inside downspouts.

Exterior. Panel design stucco; crimped lead-coated copper sheet metal; chain aluminum venetian blinds outside with inside operation; glass brick stair enclosure.

Interior. Rubber floors throughout. Acoustical ceilings. Reinforced terrazzo stair. Year-round air conditioning. Furniture, rugs, lamps, etc., specially designed by architect.

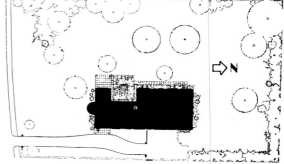

PLOT PLAN

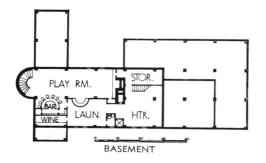

BASEMENT

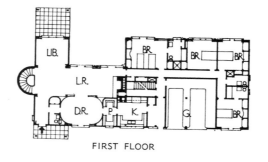

FIRST FLOOR

SECOND FLOOR

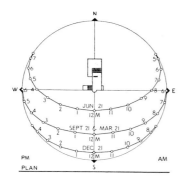

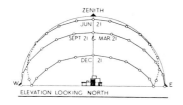

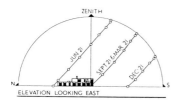

Diagrammatic Plan and elevations of the sun's path at the summer solstice, the autumnal and vernal equinoxes, and the winter solstice, shown with relation to point at center of stair tower.

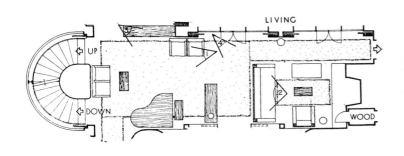

All Photos: *Hedrich-Blessing Studio*

Courtesy *Architectural Forum*

HOUSE FOR B. J. CAHN, LAKE FOREST, 1937

Family Composition and Requirements. Family of three, one daughter. Summer house; also year-round. Services elsewhere on property. Musical interests; devotion to this property; much informal entertainment.

Site. Top of small hill; 30 acres. Swimming pool.

Construction. Structural steel frame, welded. Non-bearing walls and partitions. Flat roof to carry water; inside downspouts.

Exterior. Panel design stucco. Exterior aluminum venetian blinds. Crimped lead-coated copper sheet.

Interior. Glass brick at north elevation. Plate glass to east, south, and west. Pinhole lights. Built-in furniture. Rubber floors. Year-round air conditioning. Architect designed fabrics, dining equipment and furniture.

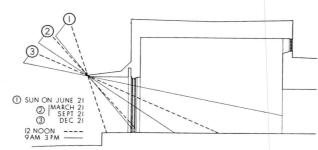

① SUN ON JUNE 21
② | MARCH 21
   | SEPT. 21
③ | DEC. 21

12 NOON ----
9 AM 3 PM ——

LIVING ROOM SECTION SHOWING ORIENTATION FOR SUNLIGHT

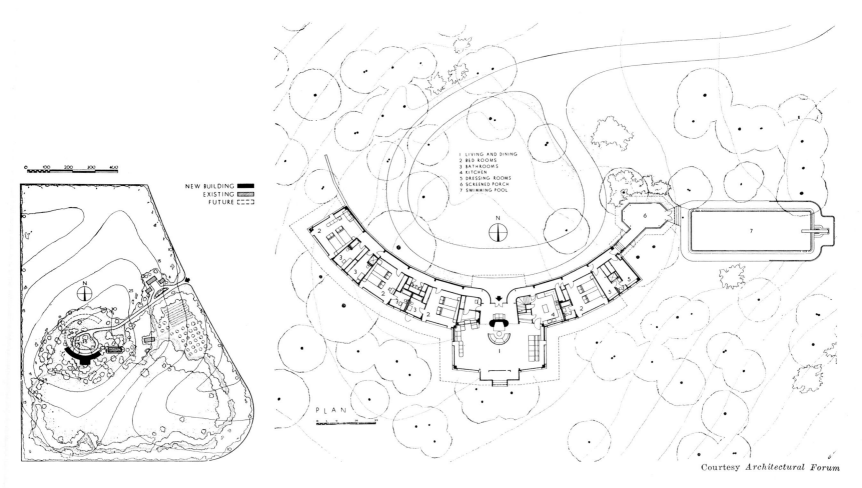

NEW BUILDING
EXISTING
FUTURE

1 LIVING AND DINING
2 BED ROOMS
3 BATHROOMS
4 KITCHEN
5 DRESSING ROOMS
6 SCREENED PORCH
7 SWIMMING POOL

PLAN

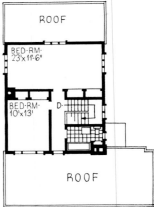

Courtesy *Architectural Forum*

HOUSE FOR WILLIAM FRICKER, WHITEWATER, 1936

Family Composition. Two people; no children. Few guests. Professional people interested in garden.

Site. Low property.

Construction. Wood frame; vertical cedar siding with battens. Exterior blinds of aluminum operated from interior. Note hoods for exterior venetian blinds.

Cost. Between $5,000 and $10,000.

All Photos: William Keck

CALIFORNIA   A. LAWRENCE KOCHER and ALBERT FREY, Architects

APARTMENT AND OFFICE AT PALM SPRINGS

Nature of Building and Site. Typical narrow business plot. Blank enclosing walls at side lot lines where, later on, adjoining buildings may cut off view, light and air.

Varied Use. Second story considered essential to insulate and shade rooms below. Offices on ground floor. Side entrance to apartment on second floor.

Climate. At beginning and end of season, September, October, and April, May, temperature varies from warm to 115°. From November on, until March, days are warm and nights are cool. North and northwest winds prevail; cool breezes almost daily. From December to February sheltered areas preferable because of cool winds. In warm weather, desirable to take advantage of breezes by cross ventilation. Kitchen location is at side where wind escapes, so cooking odors do not enter other rooms. At times wind develops into a sand storm which sweeps fine sand through every crevice. Tight construction is therefore essential, so all sash are weather-stripped with felt. Sudden gusts of wind would play havoc with large awnings, hence more sturdy shade imperative.

Construction. Fireproof. Footings of reinforced concrete. Integrally colored concrete slab at first floor. Floor covering: linoleum. First-story walls: concrete blocks with vertical steel rods every 6', tied to footing and lintels. All wall corners are poured reinforced concrete. Continuous bonding beam or lintel at plate line of exact thickness of wall and 8" to 12" in height, over all walls and over all door and window openings, forming a completely rigid frame. This special concrete framing intended as precaution against twisting and injury by earthquakes.

Exterior. Expanded metal lath and cement stucco. Roofs have 1½" insulation board mapped to steel deck of Robertson units. Three-ply built-up roofing applied over insulation board and finally a gravelled surface. Walls are warm white; windows and door frames, Indian red; railings and columns, jade green.

Interior. Cement plastered on metal lath. All floors and roofs of Robertson Keystone beam units of 18-gauge steel, exposed at ceilings.

69

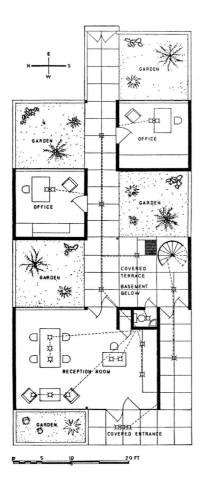

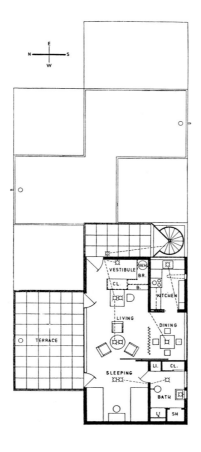

Apartment and Office at Palm Springs (continued).

Ground Floor Plan. Reception room is connected with private offices by means of a covered passage. All rooms have a glazed and ventilated wall in the direction of an adjoining patio. The side entrance leads to stairway and apartment above. Each garden plot has a sprinkler at pavement edge to produce a desired humidity and coolness, by evaporation. Almost one-half of ground floor is shaded.

Second Floor Plan (Apartment Floor). The large single-room apartment has provision for separating sleeping alcove by a sliding partition, and for giving privacy to dining space by a floor-to-ceiling curtain of oiled silk.

HOUSE FOR ALFRED L. LOOMIS, TUXEDO PARK, 1937

Requirements. Control of temperature, humidity and noise in one-story house planned to take advantage of its landscaped setting. "To verify certain air conditioning theories."

Construction. Steel and brick. Prefabricated parts: outside steel shell. Double walls nearly 2' apart. Space between ceilings and roof may be heated by plant distinct from the heating and air conditioning plant for the house interior. Use of mineral wool to deaden sound. Vibra-

tion dampers for machinery. Acoustic materials for ceilings where necessary. Canopy on terrace supported by steel I-beams.

Interior. Air conditioning machinery room, cork, insulated, in center of house. Ducts insulated.

Comments. "Two houses in one, the space between the small and the larger size house acting as a climate control zone."

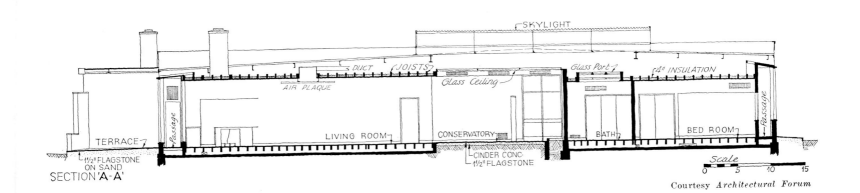

Courtesy *Architectural Forum*

House for Alfred L. Loomis, Tuxedo Park, 1931 (continued).

Canopy shading terrace on southwest corner is supported by steel I-beams.

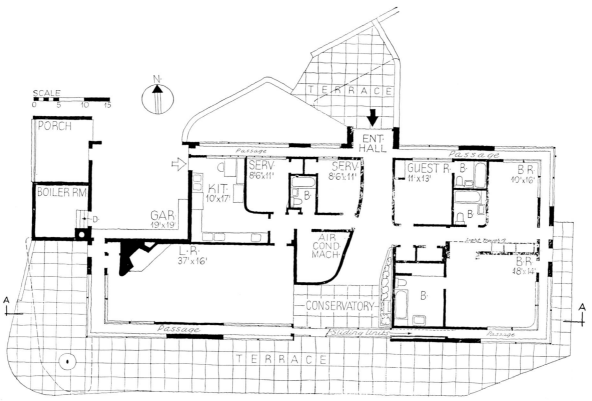

Courtesy *Architectural Forum*

View from conservatory showing double doors at right.
Blue stone slabs for floor. Walls of travertine. Ceiling
of acoustic material.

Detail of two-wall construction.

Living room corner revealing at the windows the 2' space between walls which is feature of this uniquely insulated house.

Northwest corner. Entrance and living room at right. Dining room and dining terrace behind spruce tree at left. Master bedroom and sun deck above.

West side. Covered terrace and living room at left oriented for view. Canopied entrance separated by brick wall.

HOUSE FOR
F. V. NASH, WAYZATA,
MINNEAPOLIS, 1937

Family Composition and Requirements.
Young family. Interested in art and outdoor sports.

Construction. Wood frame. Asbestos siding; partly brick. Wood windows. Roof insulated.

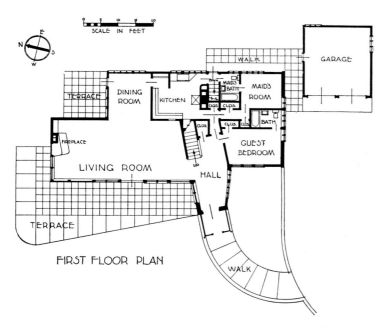

FIRST FLOOR PLAN

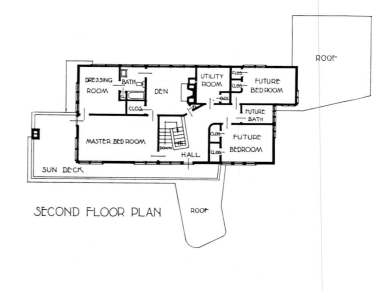

SECOND FLOOR PLAN

Photo: John Gass

HOUSE IN LEWISBORO, 1938

Family Composition and Requirements. Husband, an inventor and mathematical physicist—separate bedroom is his study; wife, a potter—her studio and kiln in basement; two children and niece; frequent visiting relative with heart ailment (dining room converted into bedroom for his occupancy); guests; one domestic. Weekend and summer use only at present.

Site. 66 acres. Owner requested minimal road, telephone and electric line expense; house therefore located about 100' from an old farm road. Grade made possible a full-story studio in basement.

Construction. Fireproof. Precast cement walls, partitions, floors. Walls of 4" solid and 4" cellular standard cement blocks, 2" apart, connected by 1/4" steel reinforcing ties. Partitions: single 3" and 4" standard blocks. Floors: precast "Floroform" joists and filling-in panels. Prefabricated parts: steel sash, rolled felt roofing, kitchen cupboards.

Exterior. White cement paint on masonry; terra cotta at west terrace; grey paint on steel sash, rails, and flush overhead garage doors; entrance doors painted terra cotta. White exterior, in keeping with neighboring houses.

Interior. Flush doors, bookcases and cabinets of birch veneer bleached and finished in colorless lacquer. Walls and ceilings: cement paint directly on cement blocks; colors terra cotta, sand, golden yellow, grey, white.

Cost. $17,000 complete including fees, but excluding road and landscaping.

Special Comments. "Patented fireproof floor construction manufactured in neighborhood; its use limited spans between walls. There are no furred spaces and, since there is no plaster, the entire structure is visible. Fireproof construction necessitated by placement of pottery kiln in the building."

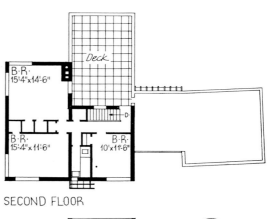

SECOND FLOOR

BASEMENT

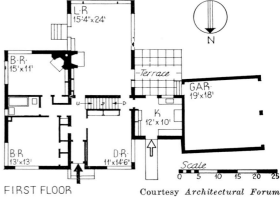

FIRST FLOOR   Courtesy *Architectural Forum*

HOUSE FOR MR. AND MRS. PHILIP B. MAHER, LAKE BLUFF, 1938

Family Requirements. Lake view, simplicity, economy, and provision for future enlargement.

Site. Three acre tract 70' above lake, heavily wooded. "As the winters are quite cold, it was considered desirable to limit the amount of glass exposure except where necessary to take advantage of lake view, and in the living rooms all exposure is concentrated in one eighteen foot window. Light is obtained by use of glass blocks on the entrance court side, which gives these rooms plenty of light, keeping them obscure from view and also minimizing exposure.

Construction. Brick veneer with wooden joists and flat gravel roof. Walls and ceilings insulated with rock wool.

Interior. Walls and ceilings: painted over plaster. Floors: oak except for rubber tile in hall, kitchen and bathroom. Metal cases and stainless steel sink in kitchen.

Comments. The second floor has been arranged with a door at the foot of the stairs so that it can be entirely cut off from the rest of the house insofar as heating is concerned, as only the first floor would be necessary for winter weekends. This arrangement provides for a house that can expand or contract for varied use and seasons.

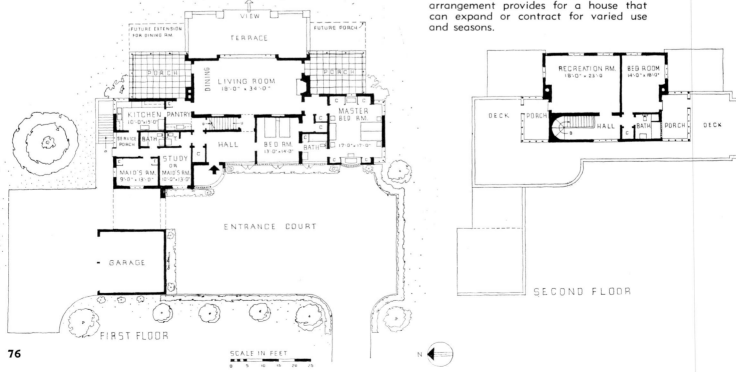

All Photos: Roger Sturtevant

Courtesy Architectural Forum

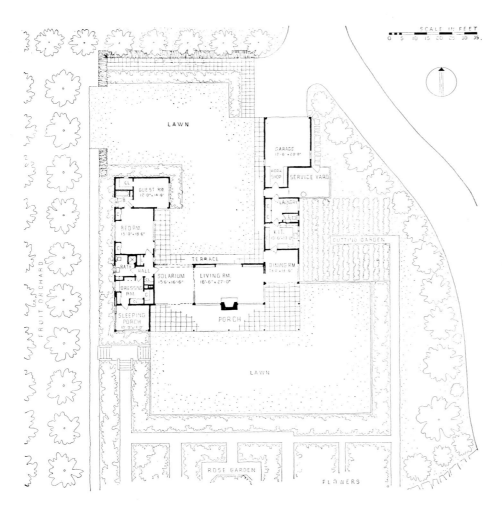

HOUSE FOR MR. AND MRS. HAROLD V. MANOR, MONTE VISTA, ORINDA, 1938

Family Composition and Requirements. Two adults who wished to acquire a new freedom of living in a house opening up to a garden that they personally would care for.

Site. Level knoll so oriented as to afford southern view of distant rolling hills, and natural privacy.

Construction. Wood frame. Redwood principal wall material used, both for exterior and interior. In both cases boarding was flush lapped 1 x 10 clear vertical grained redwood siding. Roof, red cedar shingles.

Exterior. All exterior redwood received four coats of lead and oil paint. All window sash, including sliding glass panels sugar pine. All flashing and sheet metal work copper. Chimneys common red brick. Terraces concrete, marked off in 2' squares, terra cotta brown in color.

Interior. Floors of all major rooms covered 1/4" tempered masonite in 2' squares laid over tongue and groove Oregon pine subflooring with linoleum paste. Walls of major rooms lapped clear vertical grained redwood, left natural color and texture. Walls of kitchen, laundry, and bathrooms plastered, canvassed, and painted with four coats of enamel. Ceilings of all major rooms covered with 1" insulite left natural in color and texture. Joints covered with redwood battens. Split bamboo roller and sliding screens also natural in color and finish.

Cost. $14,500.

Photos: Roger Sturtevant

All large windows and sliding glass panels are plate glass; the smaller windows in service and sleeping wings are double strength sheet glass. Sliding doors work on metal tracks with ball-bearing rollers.

House for Mr. and Mrs. Harold V. Manor, Monte Vista, Orinda, 1938 (continued).

"The house has a faint Japanese character, undoubtedly due to the sliding glass panels and to the simple form of interior design. The ceiling pattern recalls a typical mat pattern."

Photo: Roger Sturtevant

HOUSE FOR MR. AND MRS. JONATHAN H. ROWELL, BERKELEY, 1938

Family Composition and Requirements. Young couple with two children. Owners required that all major rooms face south, and that there be a quality of space and freedom through the house.

Site. The sloping site presented problems. In order to permit first floor to be accessible to the garden and garden terraces, it was necessary to enter house half-way between first and second floors. The entry hall is an enlarged stair landing. This permitted first floor to be on garden level rather than a half story above garden.

Construction. Reinforced concrete frame type of construction. The frame is unusually heavy, to be earthquake resistant. Roof flat pan tile, marine blue in color.

Exterior. Walls cement plaster, smooth texture, cream in color. Trim and gutters, redwood, painted. Sheet metal work, flashing, leaders, etc. copper. Decks and terraces of quarry tile, red in color. All glass used is plate glass.

Interior. Floors of bedrooms, bathrooms, kitchen, and pantry are linoleum. All other floors throughout are oak, stained dark. Walls plastered, canvassed, and painted. Ceilings of entry hall, library, dining room, and living room are 1" insulite left natural; walls mahogany veneer with lacquer finish.

Cost. $18,500.

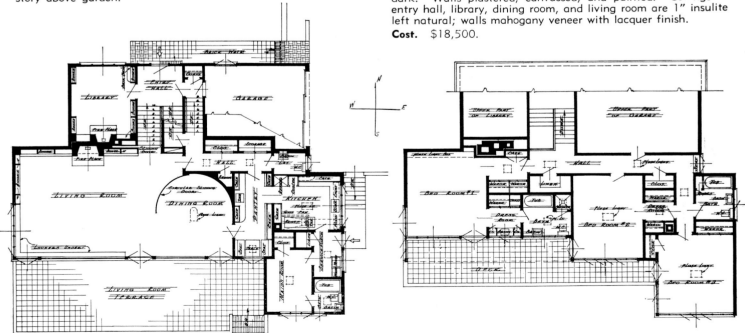

- FIRST FLOOR PLAN -

- SECOND FLOOR PLAN -

All Photos: Maynard L. Parker

HOUSE FOR MARGARET, COUNTESS OF SUFFOLK, NEAR TUCSON, 1937

Requirements. Owner desired spacious house for winter residence on the desert. Large glass areas in all rooms to take advantage of views of mountains and desert. Covered porches and roof decks for outdoor living.

Site. Slightly irregular ground between two low ridges running east and west made it necessary to level off space for house and surrounding terraces. Living room and master bedroom command view of the entire 190° arc.

Construction. Fireproof. Foundations: concrete. Floors: concrete slabs either laid on the ground or framed on open web steel joists. Exterior walls and interior bearing walls: brick. Interior partitions, and furring on all exterior walls: open web steel studs. All exterior brick walls damp-proofed on interior side of masonry with emulsified asphalt. Blanket wood insulation 4" thick in furring on all exterior walls and over all

(Continued page 81)

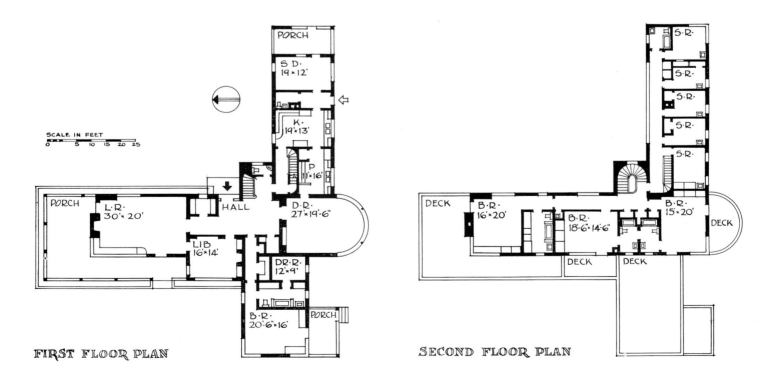

FIRST FLOOR PLAN

SECOND FLOOR PLAN

ceilings under roofs. Walking deck roofs colored concrete with waterproofing membrane. All other roofs: composition painted with aluminum asphalt base paint. Steel sash and metal door frames throughout. Exterior doors metal; interior doors and cabinet work wood. Heating: vapor.

Exterior. Finished with dash coat stucco painted a warm brown to harmonize with surrounding desert country.

Interior. Trim as far as possible has been eliminated and all built-in fittings, such as cabinets bookcases and window seats are of plain design. Doors, flush slab type with brushed chrome lever handle hardware. Walls, painted plaster, only two tones being employed throughout, a pale sea green and ivory. Travatine floors in principal rooms on ground floor. White maple floors in bedrooms and halls, and light colored linoleum floors in service quarters to provide walking surfaces which do not show the dust of the desert.

Cost. 86¢ per cubic foot.

All Photos: Geyer

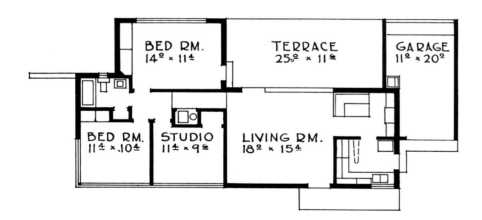

BED RM.
14º × 11²

TERRACE
25º × 11º

GARAGE
11º × 20º

BED RM.
11⁴ × 10⁴

STUDIO
11⁴ × 9º

LIVING RM.
18º × 15⁴

HOUSE FOR
MR. AND MRS. ANDREAS S. ANDERSEN, TUCSON, 1939

Family Composition. Two adults and two small daughters. Mr. Andersen is assistant Professor of Art at University of Arizona and a portrait painter; necessary to have a studio, which in order to meet FHA requirements was included as a room to be convertible into a third bedroom.

Site. Higher ceiling in living room obtained by following natural slope of the ground and by putting a ramp between bedrooms and living room.

Construction. Brick. Factory-type steel sash. Asbestos board siding on garage. All steel lintels over windows eliminated except over kitchen window; most of lintels formed out of ceiling joists. Roof is single construction. No masonry above ceiling line.

Exterior. White-painted brick. Roof: composition, white top. Rear terrace, brick laid in sand.

Interior. Walls and ceilings: smooth finish plaster. Floors: cement (not colored), treated with Repello, and waxed. Heating is forced air, gas fired. Fluorescent lighting in studio and over front entrance door.

Cost. $3.53 per square foot, including all built-in equipment.

Special Comments. "In order to allow for a rather extensive window area and yet protect the house from the hot east and west sun in summer, the eaves were given projection on the east, the garage was placed on the west end to afford the necessary protection. Due to the perpendicular angle of the sun it is not necessary to protect the south side in summer; and in winter it is desirable that the south sun enter the house in order to decrease mechanical heat requirements. The return duct of the heating plant was therefore so located that the large south window in the living room will afford enough heat in the house during a sunshiny day to heat the entire building, even in severe weather."

Courtesy *Architectural Forum*

WEEK-END HOUSE FOR ALFRED DE LIAGRE, WOODSTOCK, 1938

Requirements. House for week ends and vacation time. Owners to do own housework.

Site and Design. View to southwest determined general arrangement so that living room, two important bedrooms, and upper and lower terraces face that way. Service portions at east. Slant of roof forms high ceiling in living room (20′ x 30′ x 14′ high) and low ceiling in two north bedrooms. Attic room for a possible maid fits into northeast corner.

Construction. Foundation: concrete block. Structure: wood frame. Exterior walls: asbestos shingles. Roof: built-up and gravel, copper coping, canvas deck. Sash: wood casement, fixed and sliding sash. Interior walls: insulating board, V-joint, natural finish. Fir plywood panels. Tempered prestwood in lavatory and kitchen. Doors: flush wood veneer. Heating: heatilator unit in stone fireplace for living room and two north bedrooms. Florence heater in fireproof closet between south bedroom and lavatory.

Exterior. Light grey asbestos shingles and white trim, except trim of large corner living room window which is a strong green blue and west door in maroon. Concrete block base generally light cobalt blue; north cement terrace terra cotta color; south terraces natural grey; base under blue living room window black.

Interior. Living room: natural wood finish waxed, with blue, maroon, and orange upholstery. Grey wood-web shades. Kitchen and dining alcove: black and white. Northwest bedroom: natural wood finish with grey, black and white built-in furniture and trim, and orange accents. North bedroom: natural wood finish with deep red and blue-green trim. South bedroom: natural wood finish with white and pale lemon-yellow trim, navy blue on beds and curtain, bright Mitis-green chair.

Cost. Approximately $10,000.

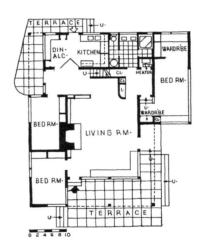

SECOND FLOOR

0 2 4 6 8 10

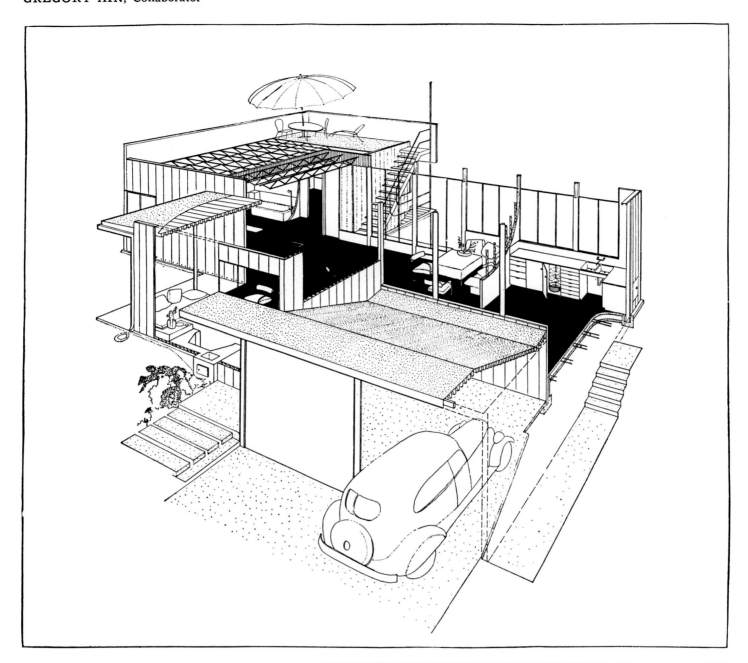

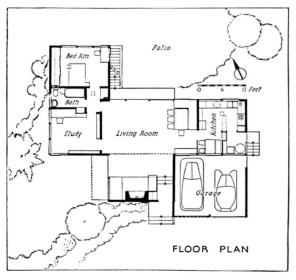

Bed Rm

Palio

0 6 12 Feet

Bath

Study

Living Room

Kitchen

Garage

FLOOR PLAN

RICHARD J. NEUTRA, Architect
GREGORY AIN, Collaborator

All Photos: Luckhaus Studio

HOUSE FOR WILLIAM BEARD, ALTADENA

"Steel-built house of 1200 square feet, with double garage. Maximum space allotted to living quarters, which by means of sliding glass and steel partitions communicate with a side and a rear patio, and to the breakfast nook and kitchen, both with broad view to the Sierra Madre mountains.

"A steel stairway leads up to a roof garden, which space may be utilized later to construct a suite of two bedrooms with bathroom corresponding to the ground floor arrangement.

"The house utilizes the standard Robertson steel floor element, also called keystone element, both for walls and for horizontal spans. The vertical wall elements erected in multiple sections are based in a typical grooved concrete footing, later grouted out with waterproof cement to produce a fixed bearing of the wall elements, which now act like upright cantilevers, and individually are designed to take lateral stresses of wind attacks or earth shocks.

"The ground floor is of double shell construction of 12" overall depth. The upper slab of integrally colored and waxed diatom cement composition is carried by cross-braced steel channel studs and encloses a plenum chamber of 6" clear depth which extends under the entire building and into which, when desired, hot air is pressed from the furnace. The diatom cement slab acts as a low temperature radiating panel during the cold season, while a retarded convection carries the air volume of the subfloor void into the vertical hollows of the cellular steel walls.

"On the building fronts which are exposed to direct sun radiation, small intake openings at the foot of the cellular steel elements initiate, simultaneously with the warming up of the exterior surface, an automatic air convection to cool these walls and minimize heat transmission to the interior caloriferic insulation board lining. The sun rays themselves operate this cooling system.

"For comparative experimentation with building economy, the roof construction was executed partly in electrically welded steel truss joists and partly in standard Robertson sections: both carrying composition roofs on insulating slabs.

"Sash are of polished cadmium steel, horizontally sliding. Exterior metal, glass, and metal-screen doors, of full room height, are horizontally sliding. Interior partitions largely surfaced with a concealed, locked, nailless, dense, panel-board covering.

"The aluminum finish on the exterior appears extremely neat and dignified, much less blinding than light stucco. The interior shell of the walls is of caloriferic insulation material and keeps conduction of heat in both ways at a minimum.

"The house was designed from the angle of labor saving. Built-in furniture such as day and night couches, drawer sets, shelving, desks, save considerable floor area and therefore cost. They also keep much of the livable area free from obstruction and thus give additional comfort. Built-in features are a carefully contemplated portion of the primary planning and of the general contract. They intimately relate to the layout of doors, windows, and fixtures, so that a complete integration of design, appearance and function is accomplished.

"In spite of the apparently large window area the amount of direct radiation permitted to enter the interior in each room is controlled by suitable roof projections and other overhangs, and also by curtains which move in a continuous curtain track.

"Hardware of sliding windows and doors, column casings, fabricated registers, etc.: chromed. Fireplace mantel: radiating bright aluminum. Floors: battleship linoleum. Walls and ceilings: sanitas.

"Kitchen with 12' white rubber drainboard, revolving cooler, garbage trap, and other typical equipment."

Cost. Less than $5,000.

House for William Beard,
Altadena (continued).

RICHARD J. NEUTRA, Architect
PETER PFISTERER, Collaborator

Photo: Julius Shulman

HOUSE FOR HARRY KOBLICK, OVERLOOKING SILVER LAKE IN LOS ANGELES, 1936

Requirements. Two apartments, facing southwest.
Site. Steep slope above road, with view over lake and mountains.
Cost. $8,500.

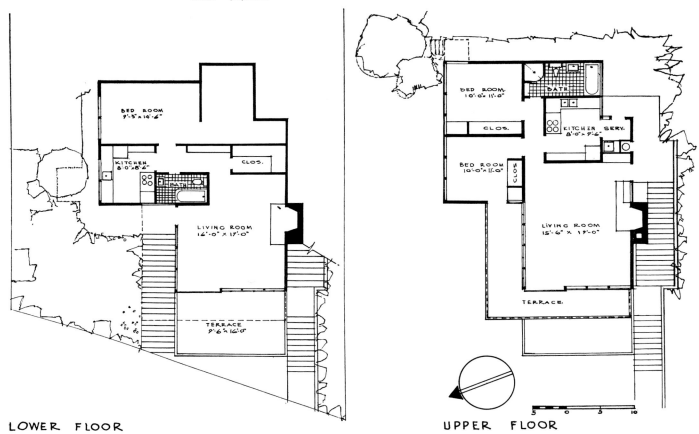

LOWER FLOOR   UPPER FLOOR

RICHARD J. NEUTRA, Architect
PETER PFISTERER, Collaborator

HOUSE FOR MR. AND MRS. JOHN NICHOLAS BROWN,
FISHER'S ISLAND, 1938

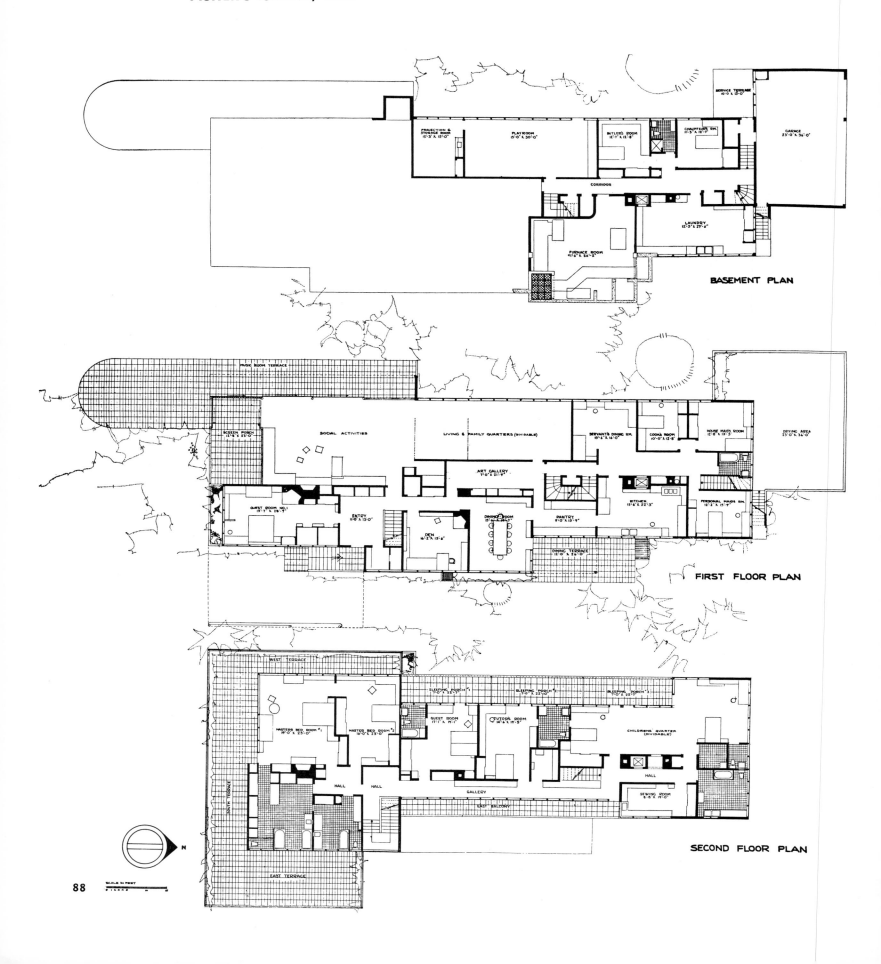

BASEMENT PLAN

FIRST FLOOR PLAN

SECOND FLOOR PLAN

RICHARD J. NEUTRA, Architect
PETER PFISTERER, Collaborator

View facing east with entrance porte-cochere.

View toward dining terrace.

RICHARD J. NEUTRA, Architect
PETER PFISTERER, Collaborator

Main view. "The light building is set off by the green of gently rising foreground lawn, a group of reddish flowering oleander shrubs, and two tall intricately branched live oak trees. The rear garden consists of a center lawn surrounded by blooming shrubbery and yellow flowered acacia trees. The southerly portion of the lot is taken up by the child's play yard and equipped with gymnastic apparatus."

View as seen from the garden. A future extension of upstairs private quarters is provided for by present deck terrace, overlooking university campus.

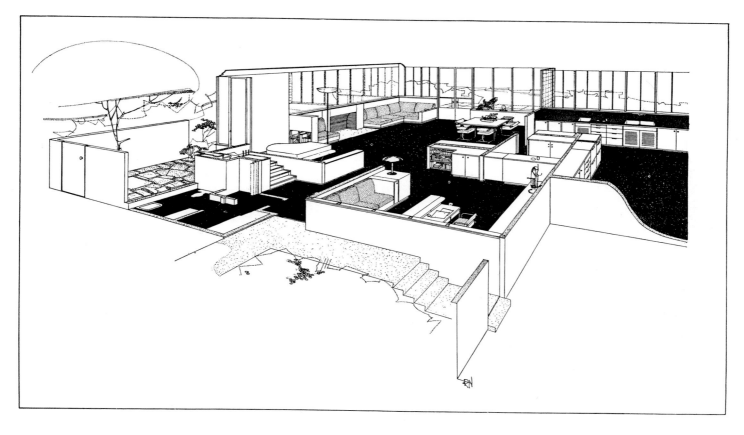

RICHARD J. NEUTRA, Architect
PETER PFISTERER, Collaborator

All Photos: Luckhaus Studio

HOUSE FOR MR. AND MRS. EDWARD KAUF-MAN, UNIVERSITY VILLAGE, WESTWOOD, LOS ANGELES, 1937

Family Composition and Requirements. Couple with one child and one servant. Spaciousness of social quarters, in spite of restricted square footage, solved by a clover-shape, three bay arrangement: living bay, dining bay, and informal den, with library, desk, bar.

Site. Slightly undulating ground.

Construction. Unit type timber chassis, continuous bracing. White cement plaster, woodwork, metal windows and sheet-metal facias: aluminum coated. Glass: plate except diffusex in extensive stair window and glass blocks in dining bay. Continuous aluminum-coated blinds permit regulation and diffusion of light influx.

Interior. "The articulated but intercommunicating arrangement of study, living room, dining room and library combined results in a spacious feeling and interesting vistas from bay to bay. The walls and furniture are of Philippine mahogany plywood. All metal trim: polished copper. A bakelite topped bar in the den, with a ceiling string of lumilines and concealed illumination in the mirrored backbar, is serviced by the pantry immediately in its rear. A large block of bookshelving separates the dining bay from this study, but no door interrupts the free flow from this room to the living bay proper and its cozy fireplace corner. A large mirror reflects the whole window front thus enlarging its visual impressiveness. A wide glass and metal door opens onto the garden patio. A special feature is the illumination of the dining space, which is spot-lighted by a built-in kliegel light, which appears as a small hole in the ceiling and only floods the table with light, while leaving the rest of the room in darkness. The floor is carpeted with a dark brown frieze carpet, continuing upstairs and thus linking the living quarters with master suite.

"Master suite with blonde bleached mahogany wainscots and furniture, indirect overbed lighting, radio and hand library built into bed shelving, extends into dressing compartment with mirror-faced partitions and swing mirror, appointed with diversified storage space, ventilated shoe closets, revolving hat racks, etc. The wainscoted, rubberfloored and mirrored master bath connects with both bedroom and dressing room.

"The second upstairs bath adjoining child's and nurse's room is similarly finished as master bath, but of smaller size. Kitchen and pantry with rubber drainboard, flush-faced cupboarding, refuse receptacle, electric range and large refrigerators, form a continuous unit from delivery hall to dining bay and extend into a maid's dining nook. Maid's room and bath, laundry and delivery entrance to the south and east."

HOUSE FOR MRS. GRACE LEWIS MILLER, PALM SPRINGS

Requirements. Small house with personal suite, and with studio (for teaching Mensendieck System) devised so that it may be curtained off during lesson hours, but convertible into a part of living room. All rooms to be easily accessible from outside. All entrances and all living to be on same level as desert floor outside. No dining room because of preference for taking meals outdoors. Open fireplace and electric heaters specified by owner for heating.

Site. Desert resort, with views to mountains and canyons to west.

Special Features. Glass window panels and sliding steel door between living room and screened porch. Wide roof overhang to protect from sun.

Owner's Comments. "Mr. Neutra's idea to make the little pool a part of the house is one of the more fortunate features of the plan; water tempers the effect of the bright sunshine and sometimes makes beautiful reflections that dance on the ceiling of living room and porch. This basin of the pool, the hearth and all the floors throughout including even the garage, are all one slab of concrete. The waxed floors look luxurious, like dark, polished marble with beautiful reflections. Floor coverings are almost altogether unnecessary, and the whole is very easy to keep clean and in order. What with the few pieces of furniture necessary to purchase; with the simplicity of up-keep; and with the beautiful completeness that comes so easily with so little care, this house has been most economical to live in."

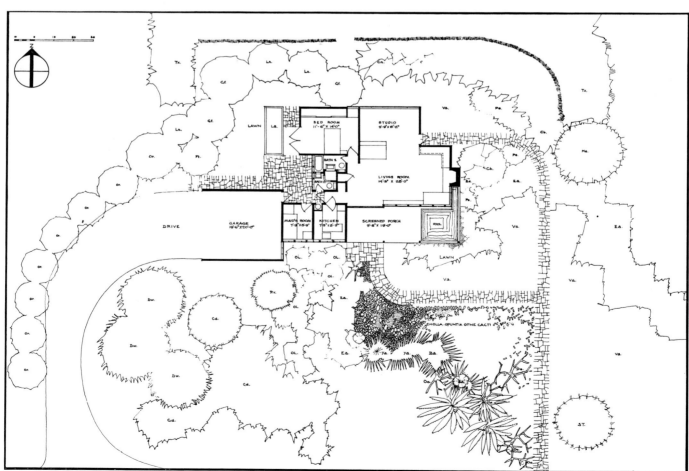

RICHARD J. NEUTRA, Architect
PETER PFISTERER, Collaborator

All Photos: Julius Shulman

View from interior, showing glass sliding panels from living
room to screened porch. Built-in bookcase and lounge.

FARMSTEAD RESIDENCE FOR MR. AND MRS. NATHAN KOBLICK, ATHERTON

Family Composition and Requirements. Parents and a son. Low-cost country house with minimum upkeep, to be managed without servants, but with sufficiently spacious living quarters to receive friends from town, and with intimate relation to the charming and quiet landscape surrounding it.

Site. Facing the coast range of the Pacific shore. Principal exposures: west for living quarters, east for service quarters.

Construction. Standardized unit type timber chassis of surfaced posts. Steel casements. Continuous diagonal trussing in vertical and horizontal planes.

Exterior. Wall surfaces integrally colored cement, smooth sand finish. Exposed steel and woodwork aluminum spray-coated for preservation and heat reflection.

Interior. Plain and simple finishes. Built-in furniture, desks, shelving, drawer sets, day and night couches, elevated breakfast nook overlooking living quarters. Air circulating heatolator. Fireplace with cushioned cozy corner seat adjoining it. Kitchen with extensive monel metal sink, garbage chute, revolving cooler. Lights are largely indirect or recessed in ceilings. Continuous homespun curtains sliding inside of window ribbons. All floors battleship linoleum.

Cost. $4,000.

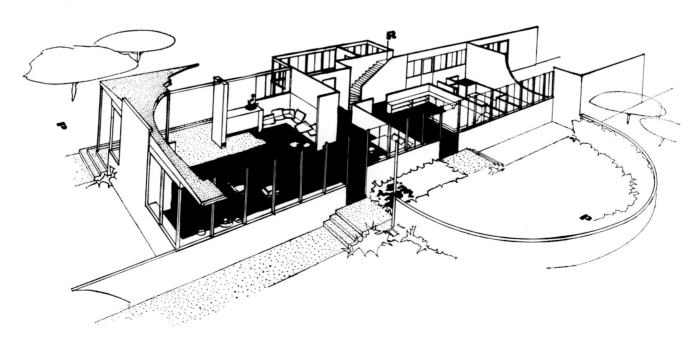

HOUSE FOR MR. AND MRS. ERNEST MOSK, LOS ANGELES

Family Composition and Requirements. Couple with adult daughter, and servant. Desire maximum labor-saving efficiency, low upkeep, and comfort at minimum cost. Five-room house on a hillside overlooking two valleys. Living room, kitchen, 2 bedrooms and bath on upper level. Private apartment with separate entrance on lower level.

Site. Main exposures: east and west; some southerly windows shaded by pergola.

Construction. Quickly erected unit type standardized milled wood chassis to fit factory made double steel sash. Continuous truss bracing below and above continuous row of windows for earthquake and tornado safety. Exterior walls steampressed composition slabs of wood shavings and cement.

Exterior. Walls below window sill integrally colored dark grey cement; redwood siding above continuous row of windows. Flat composition roof. Steel frame of windows and woodwork of exterior doors; red-brown oil paint. Exposed structural posts (between windows) and all other exterior woodwork: aluminum coated for heat reflection.

Interior. Walls of fibre insulating lath covered with pumicite coating and washable fabric. Floor: terra cotta battleship linoleum on felt. Built-in furniture: day and night couches, writing desks, drawers, shelving in red-brown stained gumwood and Oregon pine. Built-in recessed lights with diffusing lenses.

Cost. $3,500.

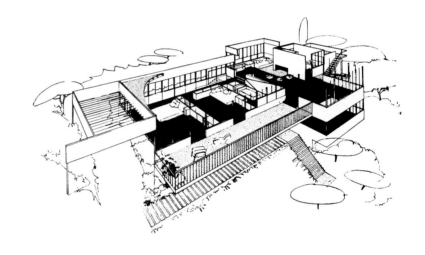

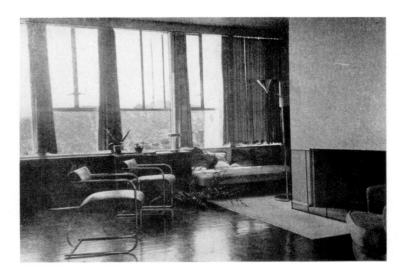

Photo: Luckhaus Studio

HOUSE FOR MR. AND MRS. ALBERT RUBEN, UPLIFTERS CANYON, 1936

Family Composition. Parents and two sons.

Site. House overhangs steep slope and overlooks wooded valley. Westerly window front commands view over ocean. Northerly front faces wide canyon. Lawn patio produced on east, by building retaining walls.

Exterior and Plan. Bonds of plateglazed steel sash and cement ribbons define exterior. Layout consists of living quarters with spacious plateglazed porch in front, and dining room with service wing, several steps higher. The lounge faces wooded Santa Monica Canyon. To southwest is terrace toward Pacific Ocean. On northeast is a landscape patio terrace with mountains as background. These fronts are plateglazed and the northeast and southwest are opened up through sliding plateglazed metal doors.

Interior. Solid walls and window parapets are flush finished with silver grey treated birchwood, as is the built-in buffet and cupboard reaching up to 4' 6", which articulates the room in its length. Easterly bay contains white lacquered round breakfast table with plain chairs of similar finish. Westerly bay has built-in upholstered seats backing against the buffet and along windows, overlooking patio and distant

Hollywood mountains. A bar counter is concealed by an electrically operated roll-down wall panel, which disappears in the basement, when button is pushed. Radio and record storage are also built in. Upholstery of natural color; drapes of same material. Floor: waxed battleship linoleum, eggplant color. Accessory metal parts are chromed. Private bedroom-sitting room is T-shaped with enlarged windowfront toward ocean. Sleeping couches in narrower inner portion; day couch, radio, easy chairs in front bay. Window drapes, on continuous track, in natural color. Walls of harmonized pastel shades.

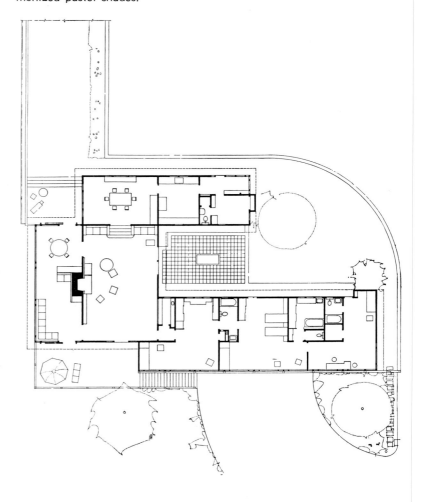

All Photos: Luckhaus Studio

Courtesy *Architectural Forum*

Entrance showing painted brick
and cypress boarding.

Photo: Paul Davis, George H. Davis Studio

HOUSE FOR MRS. G. HOLMES PERKINS, BROOKLINE, 1938

Family Composition and Requirements. Two adults, small son, two servants. Family's desire for outdoor living and dining was primary problem of architect. Dining terrace paved in blue stone and open grass terrace to be used for games were the only formally graded areas outside the house, allowing for maximum preservation of natural setting. Greenhouse also to be provided for propagation of house plants to be used during winter months. A studio, detached from the house in order to provide absolute privacy and including a photographic dark room, was also a necessity.

Site. Orientation of living and dining areas to south and west to get utmost privacy within the house and in the outdoor terrace areas. Oak woods growing over a solid ledge of pudding stone protects the house from the west sun during summer months but admits sun into living and dining areas throughout winter. Privacy is further assured by a nearly vertical cliff, about 100' to

the west, with a drop of from 30' to 40' which will prevent future building within view of the living area. Because of the solid ledge, the cellar is large enough only for the heating equipment.

Construction. Frame and brick bearing walls. Stock parts used are steel casement windows, kitchen cabinets, doors, and plumbing. Heating: dual plant with one heater providing air conditioning in master portion of house; and second heater providing forced hot water system for service portions, studio, greenhouse, and garage and as auxiliary heating system under each of large glass areas to prevent condensation.

Exterior. Finish materials of exterior are second-hand face brick and cypress boarding. Terrace over studio and garage covered with wood duck boards.

Interior. Walls of rock, lath, and plaster, painted, except in bedrooms and bathrooms where wallpaper is used. Floors of living room, dining room, and main hall are walnut parquet. Ceilings of kitchen, pantry and side halls are of acousti-celotex.

Photos: Paul Davis, George H. Davis Studio

Folding door dividing living room and dining room.

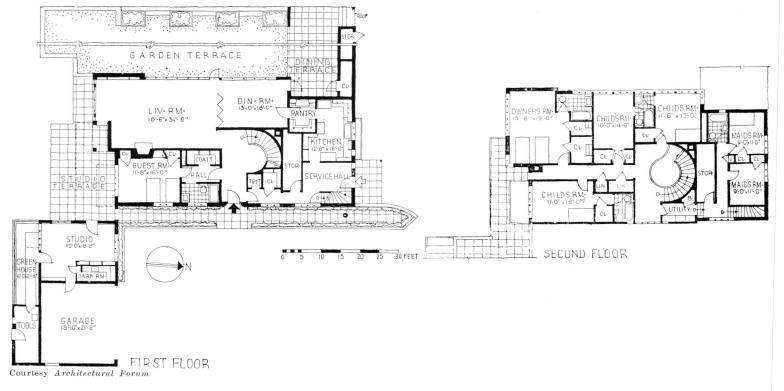

FIRST FLOOR

SECOND FLOOR

Courtesy Architectural Forum

House for Mrs. G. Holmes Perkins, Brookline, 1938 (continued).

Bridge to play deck over studio.

Courtesy *Architectural Forum*   *Photos: Paul Davis, George H. Davis Studio*

JAN RUTHENBERG, Architect
E. TUTHILL, Associate

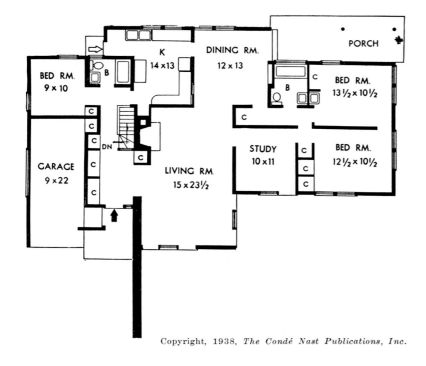

HOUSE FOR WILLARD V. KING, MADISON, 1938

Family Composition. Mother and father with 2 children; one servant.

Site. Suburban.

Construction. Stucco, frame, homosote insulation. Plywood interior walls. Gas heat. Asphalt roof.

Exterior. Stock windows of wood.

Interior. Waxed plywood for finished living-quarter walls. Closet doors of frame and masonite.

Cost. $6,500.

All Photos: Julius Shulman

HOUSE FOR V. McALMON, LOS ANGELES, 1936

Requirements. Old house to be modernized for rental purposes. New residence to be built for owner.

Site. Located on hill with steep bluff in rear, which affords a good outlook towards mountains. A small old dwelling and garages were already on the property.

Construction. Concrete basement including first floor joists of reinforced concrete. Upper structure of wood frame. Stucco finish outside and inside. Composition roofing. Deck construction: concrete floor. Sliding sash of sheet metal, special design.

Interior. Walls: yellow. Stained woodwork. Rugs: beige in various shades.

Layout. Garages and old house occupy front of lot. New living room enlarges house and serves to mask the old front. Renter has private garden. New building is placed at back of lot in order to face mountains. Instead of typical dining room the kitchen is provided with a pantry-like extension in which a dining table on wheels may be set for use in any part of the house or patio.

Comments. "Architectural scheme: the sloping roof of the old house was masked by addition of eaves which at the same time provide for the extension of life into the out-of-doors. Main building is indicated as such by means of more pronounced overhangs (13') and the featuring of the entrance at end of a long hedged approach."

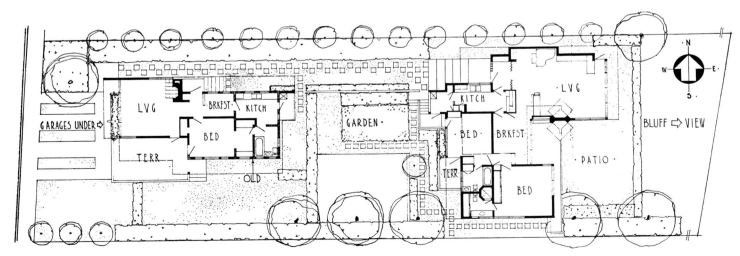

HOUSE FOR E. VAN PATTEN, LOS ANGELES, 1934

Requirements. Residence for three ladies, providing private studio bedroom for each, and community living room and kitchen.

Site. Steep downhill lot facing southwest. Good view towards mountains on left and Silver Lake diagonally on right. Directly in front of lot is an unsightly wooden roof construction covering a reservoir.

Construction. Concrete walls and beams in basement. Wood frame. Stucco finish. Wood finish of stained Russian ash. Sliding sheet metal sash.

Interior. Unit furniture. Color scheme: variations of grey.

Layout. To avoid the bad outlook in front the face of the house is closed. Each room receives two outlooks along the diagonals, one towards lake, one towards mountains. To facilitate outdoor life a patio was filled in to the level of the living room and each private room opens out onto a private terrace. These are connected with garden by means of ramps.

Comments. "Architectural scheme: Lot restrictions made sloping tile roof mandatory. The gentle slope of this roof became basis of design. Upper floor is treated as a spacial unit with the help of the converging roof lines. In order to lighten effect of roof all supporting members are architecturally suppressed and metal windows are treated as a hanging glass curtain. The architectural vocabulary is an entirely personal one suggested by the character of the owner."

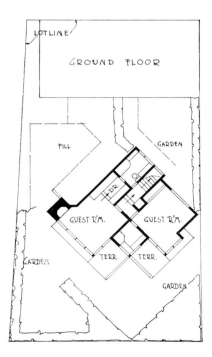

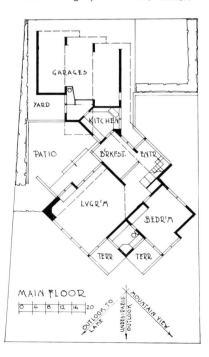

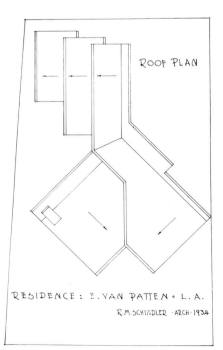

All Photos: W. P. Woodcock

Common living room for three studio apartments, overlooking Silver Lake.

GEORGE PATTON SIMONDS, Architect

All Photos: Esther Born
Courtesy *Architectural Forum*

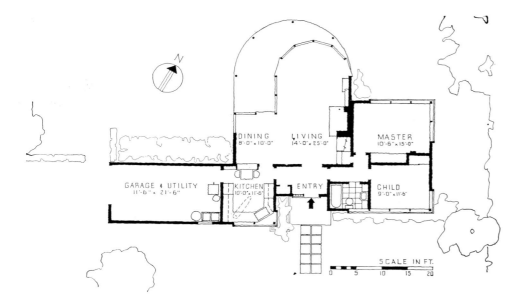

HOUSE FOR
MR. AND MRS. WILLIAM ROGER STOLL, HAYWARD, 1938

Family Composition and Requirements. Parents and young child. Ardent gardeners who enjoy living outdoors, in the privacy of garden protected from street. "Orientation, site, and family characteristics determined plan and design expression."

Site. Lot of some 150' frontage with depth varying from 80' to 30'. North boundary is tree-lined San Lorenzo creek. Bedrooms have northeast and southeast exposure ensuring morning sun. In child's room there is sun until 3 P. M. Kitchen protected from hot afternoon sun at time of day when major meal is prepared. Living room and dinette shaded by trees, so that although the glass area is large the lighting is soft and without glare.

Construction. Wood frame, Douglas fir. Floor joists are pressure treated with chemonite (copper-arsenate compound). Foundation walls: reinforced concrete.

Exterior. Walls: redwood siding laid horizontally, painted white. Roof: asphalt and gravel. House designed on modular system using 4' panel units and 4' window sizes. No plastering.

Interior. Living room walls: insulating board, screen joint construction, with plastic paint, combed, painted green; ceiling, smooth, painted yellow. Halls and bedrooms: key-jointed celotex wall panels on both walls and ceilings, painted with casein paint. Kitchen walls: Douglas fir plywood, enameled. Bathroom walls: masonite tempered pressed wood, lacquered, with chrome metal panel moulds.

Cost. $5,800, including architect's fees, heating equipment, range, refrigeration. "The economy of efficient planning and minimum circulation offsets extensive use of glass and insulation."

Windows are based on a principle of framing developed by the architect. The mullions are studs which frame through continuously (as used by Richard Neutra) but with window frames entirely outside the framework of the building which makes possible a simple and positive waterproof flashing of window frames. Horizontally-sliding wood sash.

SECOND FLOOR

FIRST FLOOR

SCALE IN FEET
0   5   10   15

All Photos: Julius Shulman   Courtesy *Architectural Forum*

HOUSE FOR SPENCER AUSTRIAN, LOS ANGELES, 1937

Requirements. Attorney, who wanted a place to sleep, relax, and play, and also a place for rental: the two units to be completely separated and with separate entrances.

Site. Lot 50' x 150' sloping downhill gradually. The only private view was to the south, so all rooms were oriented in that direction.

Construction. Wood frame. Concrete foundation. Exterior stucco. Steel casement windows and French doors.

Exterior. White floated stucco. Steel casement. Roof: asbestos deck and industrial roofing.

Interior. Plaster walls and ceiling. All ceilings covered with canvas. Wall of studio room covered with African mahogany and oak flexwood. Studio floor completely carpeted in blue. All trim inside painted in bronze. Venetian blinds, natural. Especially designed indirect and direct lighting fixtures.

Special Features. A French door opens onto a terrace and garden. A door from the living room opens onto a roof deck that can be used for out-of-doors eating. A stair leads from the deck to the garden. The second floor's hall is used as a dining room.

Cost. $5,000, including architect's fees, and built-in bookcases of mahogany, drawers, dressers, also heating, ventilating, water heater, and all linoleum.

105

All Photos: Julius Shulman   Courtesy Architectural Forum

$2,000 studio house.

HOUSE FOR MR. AND MRS. DODIE PRIVER, LOS ANGELES, 1936

Family Composition and Requirements. Studio designed especially for a young couple, two professionals. Minimum cost combined with maximum efficient space and minimum housework.

Site. Lot 50' x 150' was very steep—30' in 150'. Thus house had to be built within 5' of curb to avoid extra expense for excavating and concrete walls. The magnificent view towards Pacific Ocean and Hollywood Hills was big factor in placing house at highest point.

Construction. Wood frame, 10" T & G, redwood ¾". Steel casement windows. Heating and ventilating: wall-type vented furnace.

Exterior. Redwood planks painted with three coats of bluish grey. Fenestration: steel casement. Roof: asbestos.

Interior. Walls and ceiling insulated with ½" celotex. Plastered and canvas walls painted light cream. Ceiling painted white. All built-in furniture of mahogany in natural finish. Floors completely carpeted in beige. Dining room set: mahogany bar top finish, with satin chromium pipes. Chairs: steel tubing upholstered with brown fabric. Drapes: desert cloth, cream. Specially designed indirect light trough using lumilines.

Cost. $2,000, including all built-in mahogany book shelves, wardrobes, dressers, cabinets, and couches. All unnecessary walls are avoided thus giving a sense of space.

Comments. Due to steep slope of lot the space below the house can be utilized at any time for future expansion.

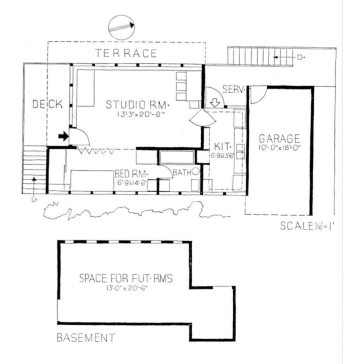

View from south of minimum house.
Cubage 6,400.

Southwest corner of multi-purpose living room: showing built-in features.

Bedroom off living room.

Dining end of living room.

Typical guest house from river side.

"MEPKIN PLANTATION" FOR MR. AND MRS. HENRY LUCE, NEAR CHARLESTON, 1937

Family Composition and Requirements. Two adults and three children. Group of guest houses for use of family and guests on and off during the winter months.

Site. Houses to open out toward river view. Formal garden walls tie the houses together.

Construction. Brick veneer, and wood framing. Concrete floors on grade; wood on second floor. Wood rafters and built-up roofing. Metal windows.

Comments. Houses jointed by garden walls and paths on one side but separate and private on other side.

FLOOR PLAN
Floor plan guest house.

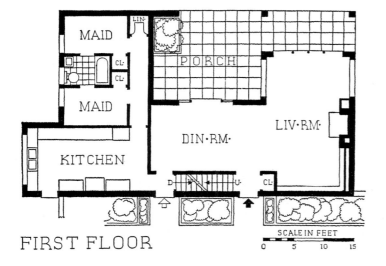

FIRST FLOOR

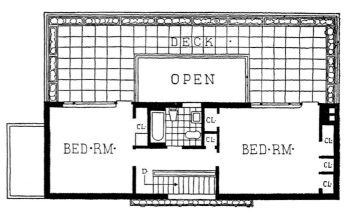

SECOND FLOOR

All Photos: Samuel H. Gottscho

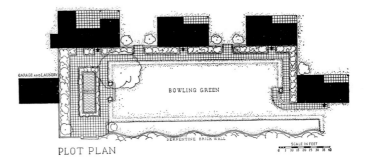

GARAGE AND LAUNDRY

BOWLING GREEN

SERPENTINE BRICK WALL

PLOT PLAN

SCALE IN FEET

EDWARD D. STONE and CARL KOCH, Associated Architects

All Photos: Ezra Stoller

HOUSE FOR MR. AND MRS. ALBERT C. KOCH, CAMBRIDGE, 1938

Family Composition and Requirements. Man and wife, one daughter, maid. Aside from usual rooms, two hobby rooms were required—one for photography and one for block printing.

Site. Small; house and garden completely fill site. Privacy for garden in city was procured by 6' wall.

Construction. Masonry exterior. Waterproof cinder concrete block walls with furring and plaster inside. Fireproof first floor; wood second floor. Wood rafters and flat built-up roofing. Metal windows. Patented cinder concrete blocks with smooth faces were laid in alternate 4" and 8" courses.

Exterior. "The large windows looking into the garden are permissible only because of privacy afforded by garden wall. The obscure glass in the dining room was used to shut out view of near neighbors while still giving light for the room and for plants."

Interior. Interior plaster is integrally colored stucco of three or four shades of off-grey, giving warmth and texture. Most built-in woodwork is Philippine mahogany. Carpets beige. Lighting largely indirect.

Cost. About $20,000 including built-in furniture.

Comments. House plan is a logical result of shape of lot, 50' x 90'; and local zoning which required setbacks from the two streets.

Courtesy Architectural Forum

SECTION "A"-"A"

EDWARD D. STONE and CARL KOCH,
Associated Architects

All Photos: Ezra Stoller

House for Mr. and
Mrs. Albert C. Koch,
Cambridge, 1938
(continued).

Courtesy *Architectural Forum*

HUGH STUBBINS and ROYAL BARRY WILLS,
Architects

Photo: Haskell

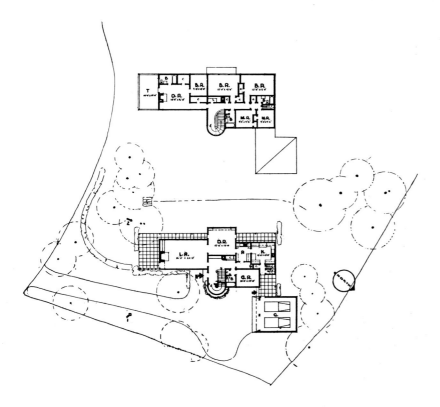

HOUSE FOR DR. F. DENETTE ADAMS, BROOKLINE, 1937

Family Composition. Doctor, wife, and two children (babies); two maids.

Site. An unopened street, all ledge. Best exposure at right angles to proposed street.

Construction. Frame. Concrete foundations. Steel columns. Roof: tar and gravel.

Exterior. Steel and wood windows. Stucco finish on metal lath.

Interior. Plaster painted, first floor. Second floor papered. Oak floors. Ice box and hot water heater combined: hot water is a by-product of the ice-cooling machine.

Cost. $17,000 including all utilities, sewer, stove, etc.

Comments. Overhang on south side to protect windows from summer noonday sun, but allow winter sun to penetrate into living room. Nurse's rooms are next to children's. All proper rooms face south to garden. Master's suite has small sleeping unit and large dressing room; also used as study.

HUGH STUBBINS and ROYAL BARRY WILLS
Architects

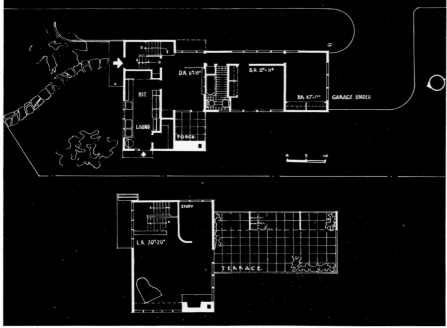

All Photos: *Haskell*

HOUSE FOR DONALD S. SMITH, MILTON, 1937

Family Composition. Man, wife, two young children, both girls. Mr. Smith a pianist and teacher of music.

Site. Sloped from street rather steeply toward the south. View of the Blue Hills possible with living room high enough to overlook surrounding houses. Lot: a parallelogram, 40' wide, 8' setback from each line.

Construction. Concrete block foundation. Wood frame.

Exterior. 3½" cedar clapboards stained eggplant color. Windows: combination steel casements with wood frames and fixed glass in wood frames. Roof: tar and gravel. Wood slat decking over bedroom roof forms the deck.

Interior. Plaster walls, painted. Ceiling, gypsum insulating tile. Floors: oak, stained grey. Fox furnace air conditioning system.

Cost. Approximately $8,000, including heater, built-in kitchen equipment, etc.

Comments. House is section study. Entrance on stair landing halfway between first and second floors. Living room suitable for a musician; opens to terrace over bedrooms.

HUGH STUBBINS and ROYAL BARRY WILLS, Architects

All Photos: Arthur C. Haskell

HOUSE FOR THOMAS TROY, NEEDHAM, 1936

Family Composition. Man and wife, young, newly married, desired accommodations comparable to a four-room apartment.

Site. Small lot but no special problem except that best orientation of living room was at right angles to the street.

Construction. Wood. Poured concrete foundation; no basement. Walls and ceiling insulated with rock-wool. Subfloor of celotex. Unit gas heater hung on floor joists; thermostatic control.

Exterior. Matched boards over heavy building paper. Windows: steel casements set into the structural uprights holding roof.

Interior. Homosote walls, painted.

Cost. $3,500. Main problem was cost; payments and expenses had to equal average apartment rental.

Comments. Minimum design for two people, one extra bedroom. Utilities and plumbing concentrated.

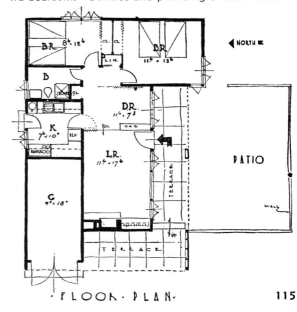

· FLOOR · PLAN ·

Photo: Roger Sturtevant

Courtesy *Architectural Record*

HOUSE FOR MR. AND MRS. FRANK J. BARRETT, SEATTLE, 1937

Family Composition. Man, wife, daughter, 2 boys, and 1 servant.

Site. Hillside plot. Sharp slope from street on west to rear of property on east. View to rear (east). Lake and mountain view. Garage to be entered from street. This condition made it necessary to avoid extreme foundations. The main floor was set down in order to place the basement level at grade in the rear, at the same time making possible a recreation area in the basement directly accessible to the yard; the main floor still being high enough to clear any possible obstruction to view. Extensive view of lake from terrace and porch at basement level.

Construction. Basement entirely concrete including first floor of precast joists and monolithic slab. Construction thereafter open stud lath and plaster and cement stucco on the exterior. Garage: concrete units 8" x 8" x 12" left exposed on the interior. Roof over garage precast concrete joists and monolithic slab, making it fireproof. Roofs: 4-ply built-up, tar and gravel. Decks: 4-ply built-up, Mastipave over. Specially designed heat and airconditioning system.

Exterior. Cement stucco floated smooth, painted white. Gutters: wood. Windows: steel, painted blue-green.

Interior. Walls: lath and plaster, painted. Woodwork: mahogany, finished natural. Floors: first floor, concrete slab carpeted; kitchen, linoleum; other floors, oak. Built-in soffit lights in living room. As west side of living room was partially below grade, glass brick was used to admit light on street side.

BASEMENT

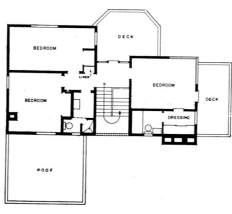

FIRST FLOOR

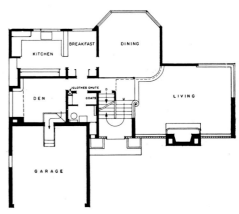

SECOND FLOOR

All Photos: Fred R. Dapprich

HOUSE FOR
CLYDE T. LLOYD AT LAKE SHERWOOD,
VENTURA COUNTY, 1938

Family Composition and Requirements. Summer residence for owner and wife. Week-end recreational facilities for son, daughter-in-law and friends.

Site. Problem: to construct on hillside with minimum excavation; to take advantage of surrounding beauty while giving privacy from highway.

Construction. Modified platform frame. Rafters ripped to form pitch and laid flat. Ceiling board applied directly to underside of rafters. Concrete pier footings; wood frame; asbestos board covering outside; asbestos board and plywood covering inside; wood sash; slab plywood doors; composition roofing and sheet metal gutters. Special framing system designed for use of lumber in even foot lengths so that stock sizes of wallboards, i.e., celotex, presdwood, asbestos board, plywood, etc. and plaster may be conveniently applied as covering, and that sash may be of 2' x 4' widths. Specially developed elastic filler to enable elimination of battens on exterior.

Exterior. Exterior joints calked and painted over to give smooth wall surfaces. Deck supported by pipe columns and covered with Pabco walking deck. Outswinging casement, sliding, and inswinging drop sash.

Interior. Heavy texture paint hides joints in asbestos walls and ceiling. Full prism glass ceiling in bathroom. Linoleum floors throughout. Heatilator fireplace. Venetian blinds. Indirect lighting throughout.

Cost. $4,200 including built-in fireplace couch, cabinets, unit tables, chairs and buffet.

Comments. "A partial enclosure and division of space by simple horizontal and vertical planes so as to provide shelter and necessary privacy and to make surrounding scenery part of each living space. Multiple roofs are like slabs of laminated rock coming out of hillside."

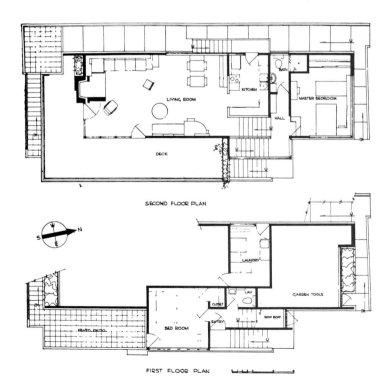

SECOND FLOOR PLAN

FIRST FLOOR PLAN

Photos: Fred R. Dapprich

House for Clyde T. Lloyd, Lake Sherwood,
Ventura County, 1938 (continued).

STANLEY VALLET, Designer   CALIFORNIA

All Photos: Alfred Cook

HOUSE FOR
MR. AND MRS. F. B. KIRKBRIDE, NEW CANAAN

Site. Uneven, hilly ground, necessitating arrangement of rooms on six levels.

Construction. Concrete blocks. Aluminum windows.

Interior. Aluminum nosings and handrail on stairs. Main entrance hallway: floor, blue linoleum; ceiling, painted terra cotta color. Living room: three walls white, one brown; ceiling grey; fireplace, grey soapstone relieved by yellow trim. Interior color scheme by William Muschenheim.

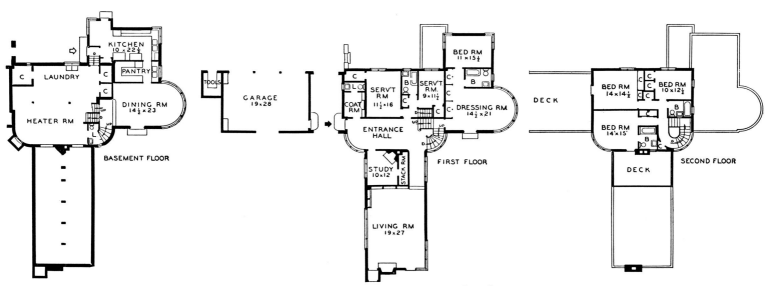

All Photos: Roger Sturtevant

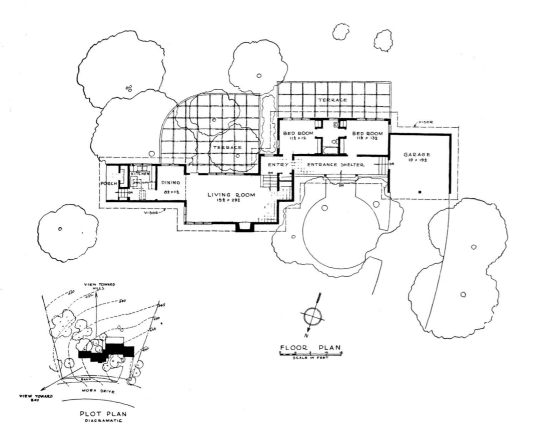

HOUSE FOR FRANK McINTOSH, LOS ALTOS, 1936

Family Composition. Mr. McIntosh and guests.

Site. (See plot plan).

Construction. "Underdown" concrete block. Continuous concrete foundation. Douglas fir roof rafters. All walls (both sides) of prefabricated blocks except certain few interior partitions.

Exterior. Warm light grey untreated concrete block surface. Sash and edge of eaves dyed black; other wood stained grey. Roof, tar and gravel.

Interior. Walls of untreated concrete blocks as in exterior. Wallboard ceiling. 12" x 12" waxed red hollow tile floor. Yellow Venetian blinds.

Comments. Permanence of structure. Ease and economy of upkeep. Ease of access to and southeast orientation of living terrace.

All Photos: Roger Sturtevant

HOUSE FOR MISS DIANTHA MILLER, CARMEL, 1935

Family Composition and Requirements. One in family. Wished to have dressing room for bathers (beach a few minutes drive); servant's room to be used by guests at times. Warm sheltered terrace a requirement. Orientation to take advantage of view and sun.

Site. Sloping site. "Long sweep of hills making anything but a simple roof line seem trifling."

Construction. Wood frame: fir studs and joists; continuous concrete footings.

Exterior. Rough redwood lapped beveled siding painted turquoise. Roof of untreated cedar shingles. Terrace: brick in sand.

Interior. Walls and ceiling of white pine tongue and groove boards, acid stained and rubbed with rotten stone, resulting in a light warm grey-brown color. Floors of 1" x 6" fir tongue and groove boards stained brown and waxed.

Special Comments. "Flexibility of living, dining room, and terrace areas."

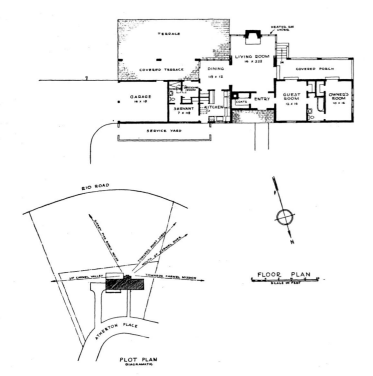

IN a movement so obviously in transition and yet so pregnant with significance and promise, there is value in capturing the viewpoints and evaluative comments of its contemporary representatives, even though they do not see eye to eye. The architects were therefore requested to send brief statements "indicating at what points American work in modern design and construction departs from European methods and may be termed distinctively American." Many complied and gave their opinions on this issue. Several have written elsewhere at length on this subject; as for example, Gropius, Howe, Kocher, Lescaze, Neutra, and Wright, and for their judgment the reader is referred to their published works and articles.

BELLUSCHI

"American methods are by habit and circumstance different from the European methods. It would not be either possible or desirable to tag a label on a country as wide and varied as America. The so-called international style must be as varied as the different landscapes and people. Regionalism in architecture has a deeper meaning than nationalism in art. If one lives in a hilly wooded country and is sensitive to it, and if he is able to shake off some of the prejudices and most of the pompousness that so far have been back of architecture, then he is bound to be in tune with certain aspects of nature peculiar to the region. If the architect with the cooperation of the client succeeds in attaining this attitude then the methods, the personal contributions, and the innovations become subordinated and are absorbed in the meaning of the final results.

"It is to be observed that many farm houses, and as a matter of fact all houses of people whose lives have been close and sympathetic to the soil, have the seed of good domestic architecture which becomes modern only because of the freedom from the artificial standards which have accumulated through many decades of superficial culture. It goes without saying that architecture when free is functional, if function is allowed to include the desire to live fully and with understanding."

DAILEY

"American 'Modern' design in larger buildings follows very closely the European, although European 'Modern' varies greatly with each country, so that there is no such thing as an exact expression of European modern.

"In smaller residential houses American 'Modern' is expressed mostly in wood—and usually painted wood, following the Colonial and Victorian tradition. This vocabulary of painted wood and painted stucco over wood frame—almost never found in Europe—seems to me to be the unique contribution of America to the development of modern.

"The efforts of our office to contribute somewhat to 'American Modern' (a very wrong name) are: 1. The elimination of unnecessary parts in detailing millwork and wood construction. 2. In the use of glazed frames, an effort toward standardization of parts, whether windows, doors or fixed glass. 3. The use of color and texture as a substitute for elaborate 'millwork.' "

DAY

"American modern usually apes European. However, different plan, real estate, labor and technical requirements produce different results.

"If my personal contribution is anything, it is in a direct acceptance of customary local methods of construction and materials, and site considerations, as something to be welcomed as helping when honestly expressed, to produce a truly functional result, rather than avoiding them in an effort to make the work look like some European structure produced under different conditions. The interpenetration of interior spaces is also a line of study to which I have devoted great thought and which is beginning to produce some individual results."

DEKNATEL

"Essentially the difference is in the conception of the relation of man to nature, or to his environment. Thus, in the modern work which has grown out of the Louis Sullivan-Frank Lloyd Wright tradition, materials are treated with respect for their inherent characteristics, whereas in the European work there is negation of material. The form which here develops from human needs and the expression of structural and material ideas, becomes, in Europe, 'pure,' an abstraction existing for its own sake inside of which the human functions are developed as a 'Plan Libre.'

"The conception of space as flowing with a ground line, wherein the architectural shelter is only a more defined and more complex part of a great continuous whole, is as foreign to European thought as their conception of space as an isolated volume, is to ours. Essentially, European Modern work is the quintessence of humanism, and, I believe, its final expression, whereas there is growing up here a new conception of naturalism, an organic architecture which is essentially American.

"Much of the European work is on a very high plane of architectural achievement. Nevertheless, it remains unsuitable to us and its importation and ignorant imitation here is no better nor different from all our preceding eclecticisms. I believe that if we are ever to make a significant contribution to world culture, it will be through the development of this non-classic, non-European philosophy whose best exponent to date has been my Master Frank Lloyd Wright.

"I hope you will understand that this is not a chauvinistic attitude toward the architecture of Europe but rather a desire to preserve intact the germ of this young American architecture which promises to be the only new thing in our world."

"I believe my work is characterized by the following: The recognition of the shelter character of building; its visible expression in the planes of floor, walls and roof. The expression of human scale: the building must create in the occupant a feeling of personal adequacy and dignity; high walls require great distances and high windows require low sills. A spacious house may have minute dimensions. Unpretentiousness: as a background to living, a house succeeds only to the extent that it helps the occupant to be most himself. A unity of interior and garden: the garden as a projection of interior space. Homogeneity: the growth of building, furnishings and garden from a single conception. Attention to circulation as the use-pattern of space. Cellular composition: the development of a characteristic cell, and the growth through simple addition of cells. This is the most flexible of composition types as addition is practically unlimited, the main stem branching as urge or exigency requires. The architectural parallel to this plant type is the Gothic in which every part enjoys a remarkable degree of freedom, and unity is achieved through basic identity of the parts; it is the contrary of classic in which there is but one life and that is of the whole. Simple regular rhythms: the repetition of a limited number of basic measurements, shapes, colors, materials.

"To realize these things in the very small house is I think a modest but real contribution to modern architecture."

"Chief contrast of American and European work and methods is: 1. American economy in labor, European economy of materials; 2. American interest in single family dwelling, 'individualism.'

"Effort at making conventional methods and materials express fresh contemporary attitude incorporating modern living techniques. Emphasis on space economies and color, texture and richness proportionate to budget."

"It seems to us that American modern design is at present distinctive from European in that it is more individual and less a 'machine for living.' Perhaps it is because our country with a wider range of climate and character of landscape than any European country must have a wider variation of design. Construction methods must vary because of the necessity of heating or cooling, etc. in different climates and because economic planning calls for the use of local materials. But we also feel that American architects have given particular attention to the demands of individual owners

HARRIS

HEGNER

**HOMSEY &
HOMSEY**

and to the aesthetic relation of the building to the site, to a greater extent than have European architects. Then there is the typical American demand for better relation of rooms in domestic planning, that is, the placing of bathrooms and bedrooms and the more convenient service layouts. Even in our low cost housing this relationship has been studied more carefully although we are disgracefully behind many European countries in the extent and social importance of this type of residential work."

KECK
"I do not think that the European approach to contemporary design and construction differs from the American approach very greatly. I stress the new freedom in planning in my office, and also comfort in the new houses I do. Comfort is very important in our vigorous northern climate, and the solving of this problem has much to do with the ultimate appearance of the house in many cases."

LIPPMANN
"Wood is cheap and the chief material of folk art in America; it is expensive and rare in continental Europe. Wood encourages retaining the bearing-wall and, accordingly, the old plan limitations; trabeation systems are apt to be rarely used except under conditions where lumber is uneconomical or the owner above economic considerations. On the other hand, the European movement has reminded us of certain amenities in living, in the joys of outdoors related to indoors, in the study of artificial and sun light and these things are influencing plan and design. Simplification of surface and sharpening of color keys has developed and the stimulus to a modern use, instead of an imitative use of modern materials is another result. Here, modern steel lintels and girders are making possible constructions which, though 'impure' as compared to the indomitable logic of the International Style, are a decent compromise between the purist independence and the classic forms. Structure, plan and appearance have been and will be affected by standardized and prefabricated parts, the minimizing of axiality, the increase of dynamic (largely horizontal) compositions, the reduction of furring and false structural effects, and the patterned contrasts of solids and voids."

MUSCHENHEIM
"American work in modern design seems to depart from European methods principally in methods of construction and in a more general use of the prefabricated materials that are at hand. It may be termed distinctively American in the results thus achieved.

"It might be stated that my personal contribution to American modern as applied to residential design has been to influence some people to accept simpler surroundings as to detail so that new groupings resulting in a broader sense of space accentuated by a free use of color could be realized."

"The proclamation that all architecture of the past was merely sculpture (Medium: Mass) and that modern architecture is concerned not so much with technic but with the mastery of a new medium of art distinct from all other arts: 'space.' " **SCHINDLER**

"I believe that the most important distinction between European modern and the more honest American functional design is that European work is an expression of the materials at hand, concrete, steel, and synthetic industrial building materials, whereas American work shows the influence of the largest building material industry, lumber. Lumber in its various forms and byproducts is readily available anywhere in the country at relative prices which almost necessitate its use." **SIMONDS**

"There is no such thing as a distinctly American modern architecture nor any other nationality. All serious works of art are international and not national. . . . The habits of individuals in different countries may color the plan; or the usage of certain standard units of construction may vary in different localities. These are only details. It does not matter whether you build with stone, reinforced concrete, wood or steel, or in what country you build it; if you are sure of the meaning of architecture and you follow a correct road without trying to be original or different, you make something of the atmosphere without embellishing it. . . . Decorations not only have nothing to do with architecture—but they weaken the forms—and weak forms never move; it is death. A good example is 'roccoco'; here form has been completely destroyed. The opposite of this is a clean, precise, orderly, not picturesque form— same as the violin stroke of a master. We never call it a French stroke or American stroke. It is a masterly stroke. They accuse us of discarding tradition! On the contrary we follow the best traditions of the past." **SORIANO**

"What can be termed 'distinctively American'? The concept of modern living and the theory of modern architecture is essentially the same that has produced all good architecture up to the period of eclecticism. The Americanization of modern design is in meeting the problems of American life. Plans are different from European plans insofar as American standards of living, habits, climate, and costs of materials and labor are different. Even in the United States architecture has perforce to be different, because of the very obvious inconsistencies of climate, customs, and topography." **STUBBINS**

"The so-called modern architecture of America, we believe, differs principally in the use of materials. The United States, unlike most other countries, abounds in stock units and sizes. Due to production these are inexpensive. Specials are expensive. The American work while enhanced by reason of, does in fact lose a certain **THIRY & SHAY** flexibility, a certain freedom, by the use of over standardization. We are bound by costs and many unsuitable materials find their way into our construction. Most of our materials are styled for styles—a fact which leads more to the curtailment of new ideas rather than to their encouragement.

"Due to high labor costs, as compared to Europe, our methods must be readily understandable to workmen and any new method, regardless of practicality, must be measured with standard practice.

"Our dwellings, for the most part, must be frame. They are subject to the vicissitudes of wood construction. On close analysis we find, under the circumstances, that a too great departure from custom is neither practical or feasible. Fundamentally, speaking in terms of costs, there has been no system devised more adaptable than 2" x 4" studs 16" o-c.

"In Europe the question is one of solving a problem in the most concise manner. Concrete is no luxury as compared to other materials. In America the question is one of solving the problem in the best manner with the materials at hand. The American public demands more equipment and the shell must foot the bill.

VALLET

"In Europe most modern residences have been built for wealthy people, while in America the majority of modern residences have been built for people of moderate means, hence in America the results are materially more related to the life of the majority and thus more representative of a nation. The important results of this fact in American design have been the utmost use of the products of modern technology, and the skilful three dimensional use of geometrical unit systems, which tends to solidify the component parts of a building into a whole unit architecturally and at the same time makes convenient the use of standard building products."

EVOLUTION AND PHASES OF MODERN ARCHITECTURE IN AMERICA

No account of the new residential architecture in America can be fair or complete without reference to the influence of Europe upon the designs of the early thirties. Many of the examples illustrated here (pp. 130-131) were widely publicized—notably those by Kocher and by Lescaze. These, as well as other experiments in the use of new materials and processes have each contributed in one way or another to the evolution of modern architecture. Some of the better examples of American houses which acknowledged the influence of French or German cubism of the nineteen twenties and early thirties deserve inclusion because, though frankly transitional, they commonly served well to acquaint the public with the new movement in architecture. The present trend is away from "the white boxes and cylinders," the corner windows, the early experimental use of glass associated in the public mind with the "modern homes" of the Century of Progress and other World's Fairs. But the experimentation in new materials, in prefabrication, and in design wnich were characteristic of this past phase played a not inconsiderable role in bringing modern architecture to its present phase—of increasing technological proficiency associated with greater naturalness of design and above all with planning that is truly organic.

1929

Richard J. Neutra. Dr. P. M. Lovell, Health house in Los Angeles. Steel skeleton; steel sash an integral part of frame. Outside shell of "reinforced concrete slabs shot through a 200' hose from an air compression gun placed on street level."

1929

Kocher & Ziegler experimented with a system of forms for the construction of "cavity walls" of concrete in the Rex Stout house in Fairfield County, Connecticut.

1930

John Walter Wood designed for Sherman Pratt at Niagara Island, Gananoque, Ontario, a house of ferro-concrete with reinforced concrete piers; floor and roof slabs integrally colored.

1931

Howe & Lescaze. Concrete house; residence of Frederick V. Field, New Hartford, Connecticut.

1932

Herbert Lippmann designed this week-end house for Frances Taussig and Eleanor Blackman at West Redding, Connecticut, of poured double-wall reinforced concrete, unplastered on exterior and interior.

Photo: Richard Averill Smith

1932-5

Robert W. McLaughlin (of Holden, McLaughlin, and Associates) as early as 1932 was designing prefabricated houses of modern design for American Houses, Inc. This is the American Motohome built at White Plains, New York, of steel frame with unpainted walls of insulating composition material.

Photo: Samuel H. Gottscho

1934

A. Lawrence Kocher & Albert Frey designed this week-end house, erected at Northport, Long Island. The light frame is borne by six 4" tubular steel columns. Wall insulation: aluminum foil to reflect heat waves.

1934

William Lescaze in 1934 and **Morris B. Sanders** in 1936 made notable contributions in remodelling city houses to ensure light with privacy on the street side by the use of glass brick. New York City.

Photo (Sanders house): Richard Garrison

1935

Hays and Simpson, ca 1935, designed this low-cost weather-boarded house of seven rooms at Willoughby, Ohio, at 32.8 cents per cubic foot.

1936

Gardner Dailey of San Francisco designed this week-end house for William Lowe, Jr., at Woodside, California. It is a three-room house of diagonal braced sheathing on fir framing with exterior of redwood siding. Interior of ¾" Greylite insulation board. Many built-in features are included. Cost $4,800.

1936

Robert L. Davison, Director of Research of the John B. Pierce Foundation, and notable experimenter in prefabrication of horizontal units, with the collaboration of John Callender, assembled two of his previous exhibition houses to construct his own house at East Northport, Long Island. Construction, 4" horizontal units of microporite on first floor and plywood covered with canvas on second.

1936

Michael Goodman designed a house in which plywood was used for exterior treatment. Home of Professor Tryon, Berkeley, California.

INDEX